T0068218

From Shattered Innocence to Radiant Healing

A Journey of Transformation Through Forgiveness and Compassion

Celeinne Ysunza, PhD

iUniverse

FROM SHATTERED INNOCENCE TO RADIANT HEALING
A JOURNEY OF TRANSFORMATION THROUGH
FORGIVENESS AND COMPASSION

iUniverse books may be ordered through booksellers or by contacting:

iUniverse
1663 Liberty Drive
Bloomington, IN 47403
www.iuniverse.com
844-349-9409

ISBN: 978-1-6632-5490-0 (sc)
ISBN: 978-1-6632-5491-7 (e)

Library of Congress Control Number: 2023913776

Print information available on the last page.

iUniverse rev. date: 05/13/2024

This memoir is dedicated to healing the heart of humanity's inner child.

"In order to recover the therapeutic magic of the theater, we must enter the theater of our own soul and become the leading actor in our own cosmic drama, allowing the eternity of the mythological structure to penetrate the chronology of everyday life." <u>Hero's Journey</u> Joseph Campbell

CONTENTS

INTRODUCTION

In silence I listen to the voices of our ancient ancestors.
In silence I watch the procession of the stars
that reveal a map of our journey.

Within this memoir lies my story of a harrowing journey as a preemie who endures abandonment, violence and abuse from Pauline, my schizophrenic, alcoholic and violent mother.

Through numerous foster homes, I was left to survive a different type of jungle, one filled with terrifying physical, emotional and sexual abuse.

Guided by grace, I found solace and love in a supportive family at the age of sixteen where I felt 'claimed' at last.

Years later as a young adult with children, I felt haunted by the ghostly scars from neglect and abuse which manifested deep within in the form of emotional and physical fragility. Recognizing my fragility, my adoptive family suggested that I consider a powerful type of transformative therapy focused on "lovingly divorcing" myself from my mother and father. The thought of anything to do with Pauline caused alarms to go off in my head as I was still feeling suffocated by a smoldering fear and hatred toward her. Trusting my new family, I cautiously agreed to consider meeting the therapist.

With gentle patience, Bob Hoffman guided me through a tunnel of transformative sessions where I was able to gradually release my deep-seated negative emotions until I became completely devoid of any feelings whatsoever toward Pauline. Feeling like a caged bird that had been set free, I felt I could breathe.

A major aspect of Bob's therapy was that I was to go to each parent, regardless of where they were in the world, and deliver my gift of forgiveness to them. Mission accomplished.

Breathing freely, I noticed a profound shift in myself and my life, much like the lotus emerging from a dark, muddy pond into the light. Serendipity followed and engulfed me as books, people, dreams and circumstances guided me forward into a lifelong study of various genres including Eastern Thought, Vedic Astrology, Western Mystery Schools, metaphysics, quantum theory and transpersonal spirituality. These became the pillars supporting my journey through self-discovery that has helped me learn to nurture the crippled child within.

I am currently living in the 'Ashram of the Elder' stage observing my contemporaries grapple with waning physical, emotional and mental health. I wonder if they have found the gateway to freedom upon the wings of forgiveness. I pray they have as we are each working collectively on behalf of all mankind.

Imbued with the spiritual wisdom of samsara, the laws of karma and, especially, the profound sanctity of every person's presence in my life, including the good, the bad and the ugly, I reflect on Pauline's life of deep mental torment. My wish for Pauline is a peaceful-heart closure through both hers and my forgiveness toward each other.

With self-forgiveness I acknowledge my own inability to be strong enough and courageous enough to be there for Pauline, especially during her painful transition. Understanding the Oneness of mankind, I see how we choose our parents and the accompanying scripts with specific lessons to fertilize the soul. There is a saying: "You are [an aspect of] me. I am [an aspect of] you."

Wherever we seek divine answers and guidance we can see that all rivers flow to the Sea of ONE consciousness, that of a higher realm.

Forgiveness and compassion for all, knowing we are each other in some miniscule way, truly expands the heart with gratitude. Gratitude is the magnet that attracts greater abundance of life.

Am I complete? Of course not. As the song says, "We've only just begun." There is no ending, only perpetual journeying. Step by step, together we climb shoulder to shoulder toward the Apex at the top of the mountain.

Breathe in gratitude. Exhale forgiveness into the heart of mankind. We are still very young children of God. Nurture yourself with compassion and forgiveness.

ABOUT THE AUTHOR

A lifelong seeker and student with a highly curious mind about the how and why of life's dramas and traumas, Celeinne immersed herself in traditional studies, but felt most drawn to more philosophical and esoteric venues for answers that have proven to resonate more deeply within.

To this day, she credits Bob Hoffman, of The Hoffman Institute, for his powerful one-on-one processes which set her soul free from intense hatred and anger toward her birth mother to travel the path of 'becoming' an aspect of compassion and forgiveness.

Celeinne's fifty plus years of studying Eastern Thought, Western Mystery Schools, Vedic Astrology, quantum theory and metaphysics culminated in becoming an Ordained Minister with a Doctorate Degree in [Metaphysical] Philosophy, specializing in Transpersonal Consciousness through the education department of the University of International Metaphysical Ministries in 2010.

As a spiritual guide, Celeinne shares her knowledge of studies together with breathwork and prayerful meditation as well as the therapeutics of writing and mandala-drawing as taught by the late Judith Cornell [Dr. Rajita Sivananda].

In addition, Celeinne is a vibrational sound practitioner using the Soma Energetics' vibration and body tuning forks.

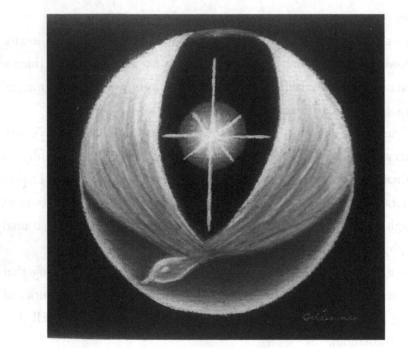

CHAPTER ONE

Whisperings Within an Echo Chamber

As my husband handed me the package he had retrieved from the mailbox my heart twitched like the last spasm of someone taking their final breath.

With a life-spirit all its own it sat on the counter waiting. I felt its eyes following me. I was sure I caught a fleeting glance of slow rhythmic breathing.

Testing. Testing. Testing. How much progress have I really made in my intense desire to throw off the shackles of bondage to this endless nightmare?

Like the immediate snap of a dry twig under foot, the floodgate holding back a torrent of heavy murky waters pressed forth violently, demanding to be opened and relieved of its painful pressure.

Three days later I mustered the courage to open the little package which contained a charm bracelet of beautiful blue chalcedony, an elephant and a heart-shaped watch. No written message. One lonely bracelet waiting to be claimed.

As had happened often before and was occurring more and more frequently, I suddenly felt myself being swiftly sucked into and tumbled about in that all too familiar suffocating vortex.

Confusing words echoed from a place of all-space and no-space, simultaneously. They seemed to be coming from yesterday meeting themselves as in a mirror from tomorrow in an exchange through the moment of today.

'This bracelet is merely a symbol, a very limited outward expression, of the greater gifts that have become silenced by the intense glowing embers. These are the gifts that have been crying out to be released by the gift of breath to rise once again and become part of the serpent's mesmerizing dance in the brilliant flames'.

This message, like so many before, resonated through every cell of my being like a shimmering strand of DNA. Mysteriously necessary?

Most unexpectedly, the formless ghost of dark night draws me out to dance with him in a tantalizing symbiotic waltz while the village sleeps peacefully. One, Two, Three. One, two, three. Together we float in perfect rhythm.

Where do these ideas or messages come from? Why do I always feel the presence of a tall powerful force standing over me whispering these thoughts which usually seem incomprehensible to my intellect yet somehow resonate in my heart to soothe me like cool running water? How can this be both unsettling and calming in an oxymoronic way?

CHAPTER TWO

Viewing Through a Rearview Mirror

As though straining through a rearview mirror to see where I had been, I see dimming scenes that appear darker, harder and harder to see clearly, like the light bulb slowly losing its wattage.

How far back can we 'consciously' remember? Are there memories etched somewhere within even if we cannot remember them? It is believed in Eastern and metaphysical circles that there is an indelible record of the all-time for each of us and for us as a collective whole entity. Past. Present. Future. All these states are the same without differentiation say the ancient seers and holy ones. It is our perception that distinguishes them.

When I ask myself what my very first memory is, it seems like I am looking back through a long radiant tunnel of a rosy, peachy color that curves slightly to the right. Nothing as concrete as a physical body is revealed. Rather, I 'feel' a strange sensation of cold, a sensation of hardness and a feeling of suffocation. My guess is that maybe it was an overwhelming response to the oxygen mask that was keeping me on life-support. I was born two months premature, weighing two and one-half pounds. Although I vaguely remember my aunt Ginny from when I was very young it was not until I was fifteen when my aunt came to California to visit that I learned the details of my birth. The story from my aunt is that nobody knew Pauline was pregnant. She was anorexic because she lived on Camel cigarettes and Four Roses bourbon, never showing any signs of pregnancy. I was her very well-kept secret.

Pauline's sister told me how Pauline appeared at her doorstep one day with this little pink 'thing' that looked like a wad of chewed-up bubble gum. Pauline explained to her sister that she had just picked me up from the hospital after waiting a couple of months for me to weigh up to five pounds before I could be released. Pauline told her sister that she would be back shortly to get me.

My aunt told me how I had to be rushed back to the hospital emergency twice shortly after Pauline left. The first time was to be treated for pneumonia. The second time was because my cousin who was five years older opened the baby bottle and poured formulae into my mouth to get me to stop crying. For weeks Pauline was not heard from, nor could anyone find her.

A couple of months later my father, Frank, appeared at my aunt's door looking for his wife, Pauline. He had been off at war. Aunt Ginny told Frank that she had no idea where Pauline was and invited him in to meet his daughter. He didn't know that I had been born.

In contrast to zeroing in on a 'sensation' as my possible first memory, I do remember clearly the time of being a toddler lying curled in the fetus position so my body could fit into a tiny baby crib that my developing body had outgrown.

It is with clarity that I am aware that this memory remains strongly imprinted somewhere in an archive of my consciousness because it is an adjunct to something far more memorable or painful than my body being cramped in a crib inside a tiny apartment with Pauline and her boyfriend, Joe.

The radio was on. Pauline and Joe were listening to a baseball game in another room. The voices of Pauline and Joe became louder and louder. Anger was clearly the tone and timbre of the voices.

Suddenly the radio was drowned out by the loud crash of shattered glass followed by a very loud bang. Panicked with overwhelming fight or flight syndrome, I was fueled with the necessary power to scramble over the top of the crib.

Pauline yelled out to me from the other room to "RUN"! Etched clearly is the memory of the immense, hot energy of fear that seemed to lift me and, in an expanding velocity, seemed to carry me effortlessly and swiftly to the door of a neighbor downstairs where I felt momentarily safe, though still alone and terrified. What happened after that?

A deep sleep rushed in to rescue me with no recall of the aftermath of that event. Over the years I found that I would automatically go to sleep quickly to block out traumatic situations.

CHAPTER THREE

Nature's Embrace

The next memory that played out seemed like a remote scene in a movie. I was sitting on grass under the warmth of dappled sunlight, feeling the peaceful beauty of being kissed by a gentle breeze and of being celebrated by melodious songs from the birds nearby. What is clearest is the memory of a totally unknown sense of feeling safe and loved. It is incredible how clearly this has remained with me all these years, as precious as a rare gem from earth. The intensity of this feeling was greater than the intensity of the opposite feelings of terror I had felt at times previously.

This was during a very brief visit with another aunt and cousin sometime before I was school age. This was the only time I felt safe and loved as a very young child. Aunt Helen's voice and touch were warm, soft and comforting. I could feel her acceptance of having me there with her. She gave me her undivided attention and support to explore the surroundings of her home and flower garden. My cousin, Bill, was a teenager who treated me like I was a little princess, indulging me lavishly. Bill loved to show me his model airplanes that he had put together and hung from the ceiling in his bedroom. He also had a chemistry set which he warned me to not touch or play with. Amusingly, I remember putting his chemistry tubes down a hole somewhere. Best of all was when Bill would fold me into his bicycle basket and ride all around the neighborhood. The bumpy ride with the wind in my hair was heavenly. I wanted to never leave them.

However, my life seemed to be a leaf swept along with a swift current in time rushing to merge with the unknown mysterious river of life. I don't remember if Pauline took me from there or where I went next.

'*Yes, you are* making progress for as the Zen saying goes, we can see our reflection clearly only when the waters are still.' In the Bible is written, "Be still and know that I am God."

These words inside my head were more frightening than comforting.

CHAPTER FOUR

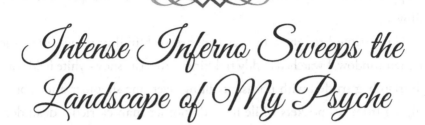

Intense Inferno Sweeps the Landscape of My Psyche

Around the age of six is buried another treasure chest of memories; memories of feeling safe in a little two-story, two-bedroom house with a well to pump water, an outhouse and a chicken coop. A large wooden barrel collected rainwater at the end of the porch. We grew our own green beans, peas, carrots, potatoes and tomatoes. I remember stringing beans before they could be canned. The huge, ugly potato bugs in the ground totally spooked me. Together we set out scarecrows to chase the birds away.

We picked luscious red and green apples from an orchard below the house. At one end of this immense property were wild black berries, raspberries and blueberries. We raised chickens. It was a real treat to have fresh chicken and dumplings for our Sunday dinner although I couldn't stand to watch while the chickens were flung in a circle to wring their necks. This was our Sunday ritual. I felt sad that mom spent what seemed like hours tweezer-plucking the feathers that remained after boiling the chicken. She seemed to work hard every day and never seemed to laugh or be happy. Her sadness was reflected in my heart. I yearned to comfort her with hugs because I recognized her pain in myself. Maybe I was wanting to comfort myself. However, she was like a dour robot who mindlessly executed her chores without showing any emotion or warmth.

When I accidentally put the very hot iron on my hand, causing puffy

9

blisters almost immediately, Mom impatiently stopped her chores which seemed to forever consume her, to put butter on my blisters. She then told me to go upstairs. There was no eye contact. No hugs. No expression of warmth or concern. I felt relieved to be able to leave her line of sight. Wrapped in the fluffy down comforter on the bed, I cried quietly into my pillow.

Wintertime brought a forever expanse of blinding snow. From the kitchen window, I watched daddy trekking across the snow-white field with a burlap bag stuffed with pheasants flung over one shoulder and rabbits bulging from his pockets while he and another man carried a dead deer suspended from a pole on their shoulders.

Leaving through the kitchen door across the porch to walk to school, I came face to face with the deer. Its big dark eyes were still wide open as it hung lifelessly on the porch. It made me want to cry and throw up. The fact that it was the necessary meat for us to survive didn't make me feel any better for the deer that didn't escape the hunter's bullet. We had no refrigeration so the meat, along with the garden vegetables and fruits, were canned and stored in our root cellar.

Our little two-story house with bedroom dormers stood naked in an expanse of space not far from a thick forest. Neighbors on either side were situated several fields away from us. It was peaceful living on the land. The apple blossoms were beautiful to watch as they bloomed slowly on the trees like a symphony coming to life. I loved to go into the forest and listen to the birds chirping and the chorus of various critters. The lovely green moss I collected dried and turned brown shortly after I had taken it to my bedroom. Although I didn't feel the warm feelings that I had felt with Aunt Helen, I did feel safe. I felt there were angels present, wondering if they revealed themselves as fireflies.

Life at that time and in that place was like an idyllic scene from Norman Rockwell. There were no paved streets or sidewalks, only dirt roads. The one school was a little red three-room schoolhouse within a hearty-walking distance. Grades one through three were in one room, grades four through six in another room. The principal's office was in the third room.

Out-houses were fenced behind the schoolhouse. The steeple on top of the building held the school bell which we got to ring by swinging on the rope. We cleaned the felt erasers from the blackboard by pounding them against the side of the schoolhouse. With squeals and giggles, we pounded out frantic rhythms as the chalk dust dissipated into the air. Such fun.

Behind the schoolhouse was a train track. During recess I would look forward to watching the train go by because daddy was the conductor. His train rolled through during our playtime outside. Daddy would always blow the whistle and wave a white cloth if he saw me on the playground. I felt proud and special at this little private ceremony which only I had of all the school children.

We lived our lives in this little country town almost exactly like the song we sang in the classroom. 'This is the way we wash our clothes' as the song went. Each day was a different chore for mommy, just as the song was sung. I remember Thursdays best because that was the day brother Billy and I awoke to the aroma of yeast rising and bread baking. I longed to stay in bed all day with a book and breathe in the delicious smells. Heavenly.

Suddenly, a part of me died one thunderous night, shredding the chapter of this storybook Norman Rockwell town.

A terrifying internal hurricane of flames burst with full force into my heart and psyche scattering shards of panic, fear and despair. There was no place to run. It began with the setting sun of growing darkness and the roar of rumbling thunder when daddy turned off the lights in the living room where he, brother Billy who was age three, and I had been sitting listening to music on the radio. Billy had fallen asleep on the couch. I went to my bed upstairs. Thunder and lightning had always made me feel nervously unsettled. So powerful. Mommy was gone for the evening. It usually took me awhile to escape the fright into a liquid dreamscape of luminous colors and angels with transparent wings.

This night, however, I was suddenly ripped from this state of dream-sleep. Sensing a dark presence, I awoke to see daddy's hulking figure over me. Despite the booming thunder, I could hear that his heavy breathing had a slight wheezing sound. The flash of lightning revealed a face I did not recognize. RUN! My muscles seem to be screaming at me. Frozen with fear and pinned down physically with his hand over my mouth, I could not run. Unable to move physically, I wondered how to get myself back into that dreamscape; how to truly become invisible and throw off the coarse burlap robe of sickening fear and shame.

Feeling lifeless and frozen I fell into a deep sleep as though I had been chloroformed. What happened next? I do not remember.

Early the next morning I searched deep into mom's eyes for a safe harbor to provide comfort. I was desperately needing to be held close. As usual, her eyes didn't meet mine. I was hoping that somehow, some way, she would sense my frantic need to connect with her. She always seemed to be not present, and this time was no exception. She simply wasn't ever present. I had become all too familiar with the strange sensation of feeling invisible. Feeling like I was suffocating with fear and sadness, I reluctantly walked out the door into the cold along the lonely dirt road to the little red schoolhouse.

Closing the door behind me from our house I felt like running to somewhere far from this house and town, but to where? We lived in the middle of nowhere. To whom? I didn't know anyone other than Pauline whom I feared most. Besides not knowing the whereabouts of Pauline she was the last person with whom I wanted to be. I just wanted the feeling of safety that was there until the night before.

Inside the cozy little red schoolhouse with a wood stove and school desks with ink wells perfectly placed into rows, I slid onto the seat of my desk and tried to busy myself by lifting the writing portion to fiddle with the pencils that were stored inside. Numb, tired and confused, all I could do was swallow hard to keep from screaming and throwing up.

School was something I enjoyed. Learning new things always interested me. I looked up to my teachers with respect, thinking that I would grow up to be a teacher. This day, the teacher's words were silent to my ears even though I saw her lips and body move as usual. Like Alice stumbling on a rabbit hole, I felt myself spiraling downward into a dark vortex with the realization that there was no escape route or safe harbor. There was only a feeling of being suddenly dropped all alone onto a vast expanse of a dry lake in the dark of a moonless night.

Recess time at school. Hearing the whistle of the approaching train, I chose to cling to my school desk rather than run out to meet daddy. I just couldn't muster the strength or courage to act out the private ritual we had shared. It no longer felt like it was special for me. The full reality that he was not my 'real daddy' sat on my heart suffocating me like a heavy boulder. I knew they were not my real mommy and daddy, but it felt so comforting to be able to call them mommy and daddy. I no longer felt safe. I no longer felt I was theirs. I felt dirty and ashamed. I felt totally alone, frightened and suffocating with fear and sadness again. I felt like I no longer had a family or a home to turn to. My time there was probably less than one year.

The teacher noticed that I had remained seated at my desk during recess. Too frightened by the thought of going home after school, I told my teacher what had happened, hoping she would rescue me. She didn't. She listened very calmly, asking some questions and then told me that I had to go home at the end of class that day. She left me sitting there feeling stunned and all alone for the remainder of the recess. She turned away from me and left the room. Fear and confusion consumed me, wondering if she didn't believe me or care at all that I was too afraid to go home.

To escape the all-consuming flames of emotions that engulfed me, I practiced writing cursive letters over and over on the lined writing paper.

Somehow the rhythm of my hand flowing through the shape of the upper-case letters' "*E*" and "*S*" over and over was soothing. When recess was over, the teacher returned to resume class for the duration of the school day.

The next day when I returned to our home after school, I was surprised to see daddy there. He didn't usually get home until around dinner time. He looked larger than he really was, dark and brooding. Mommy said that the teacher had called her the day before. My heart skipped a beat and then began to race. I feared mommy and daddy may be able to hear my pounding heart. I knew I had not been believed by the teacher. Daddy's piercing look and mommy's tone confirmed that no one believed me. I felt myself being sucked into that dark vortex again.

Suddenly, from nowhere, daddy pulled out his leather razor strap empowering life into it as he swung it all over my body like a possessed snake in a wild frenzy of anger "for telling such a big, nasty lie." Mommy turned on her heels and left the room. More than the physical pain of the razor strap, I felt as though I was going to die from my feelings of abandonment, vulnerability and great danger. Numbed with shock, the welts and tiny abrasions on my body, I felt I didn't dare cry for fear it would make daddy angrier.

Following the drama in the kitchen with daddy and mommy around what they considered my 'big nasty lie', I felt a presence of a different kind that night. This time there was nobody of a physical nature. Rather it was more of a light glow from which a symbol slowly emerged that I could not comprehend. There appeared the symbol of a square with a circle inside. Each seemed to be alive, slowly moving in the opposite direction to each other. This cryptic symbol confused me and caused me greater anxiety. Exhausted, I fell into a deep sleep without the usual tossing and turning to try to not see the lightning and hear the loud thunder.

How many days after that did I find myself waiting at the window, suitcase packed, for Pauline to come get me? I cannot recall. She didn't come that first night. I took my pajamas out of the suitcase and crawled into bed.

The first night was to be a rehearsal for the next several nights. The intense silence that resonated throughout the house was terrifying. There was not even any sound from little brother Billy's presence. No one spoke. We ate dinner in silence after which I went directly to bed.

I don't remember going to the little red schoolhouse after that. Each day I would stare out the window for what seemed like months waiting to be retrieved by a woman whom I did not really know, with whom I did not feel at all safe and with whom I did not want to be. She was the lady who gave birth to me, but not once could I ever consider her or address her as my mother in any sense of the word.

Eventually, I heard the distant hiss of the bus door open though I couldn't see it from the window. I knew it had to be the delivery of "her". This was the first time I had realized that a bus came here. Nobody came to this desolate, out of the way hellhole by bus.

Tall and slender with an air of arrogance, I saw the kelly-green-suited lady approaching our house. Her lacquered blonde pompadour hairdo made her look even taller and accentuated the features of her high cheekbones and ruby-red cupid lips. On the dusty dirt road, she walked in high heel shoes maintaining excellent balance with an air of elegance. Pauline looked completely out of place. As I watched her approach the house my head began to pound, my eyes ached from the light and my stomach began to roil. This was the beginning of years of experiencing debilitating headaches.

Her steely blue eyes glared angrily at me as she crossed the threshold into our tiny kitchen from the back porch where daddy used to hang the deer in wintertime. No smile. No hug. Mommy gave me a little shove on the shoulders as she told me to go upstairs to my room.

After a brief exchange of mutterings, I was called to come down with my suitcase. No goodbye hugs. Only a terse yank on my wrist. Attached to Pauline like a lifeless cloth doll we went out the door to the dirt road where the bus stop was. I was terrified of the unknown that lay in waiting before me.

Pauline and I boarded the bus for some unknown place. It seemed we were the only two passengers. Chilling silence was permeated with flashes of cold, angry steely-blue eyes cutting through me again. I felt like I was spinning uncontrollably in and out of a body fluid dream-state, hoping I was as invisible as I felt I needed to be. Surreal. How long was the ride? Where were we going? Was I to be once again trapped inside a cage with this volatile stranger? Or would I be lucky enough to be once again dropped on a stranger's doorstep like an abandoned puppy or kitten? I could only hope so.

Years later I received a letter postmarked Pennsylvania from mommy's sister, whom I barely remembered. It was addressed to Pauline who forwarded it to me wherever I was staying at that time. She wrote only that one time. It was very strange to get a letter like this and even more strange what was written. Enclosed was a picture of Billy and a brother who appeared to be a few years younger. Between the two brothers was a little blonde girl, named Carolyn. Apparently after mommy and daddy had another son, they decided to adopt a girl child. I felt my breath suddenly stop and my heart pound. I wanted to scream out to that little girl to run. I couldn't believe they had adopted a very young girl. But what bothered me most was that I was hearing from a woman I barely knew or remembered and that it seemed her purpose in writing to me was to showcase mommy and daddy's children. Why? To this day I cannot understand how they could have been able to adopt a girl and why mommy's sister, whose name I don't remember, felt the need to write to me.

"If our children are to approve of themselves, they must see that we approve of ourselves". Angela Mayou

CHAPTER FIVE

Broken Swing

Flying higher and higher on the playground swing gave me a sense of euphoria. If only I could fly out of the leather seat into the vast expansive sky to never return.

Suddenly brought back to reality, Penny's voice called me from the stately white house veranda. I had been living at this state-run home in Pittsburgh with about 36 other girls. I think this is where Pauline left me after taking me from mommy and daddy's house in the country. For how long I was in this home, I have no idea, but I think it was one school year. I was one of the four youngest girls who shared a bedroom. Although it was a highly structured regime, I found it to be at least peaceful and even fun with the other girls as playmates. More importantly, I felt safe.

Penny called my name again across the grassy playground. My feet dragged, acting as brakes to slow the to-and-fro action of the leather swing-seat. Walking across the grass to the big white house, I wondered why I was being summoned to go in.

I entered the large formal parlor with its high ceiling, mahogany wood walls, doily-covered furniture, huge marble fireplace mantle and the oversized 'umbilical cord' spindles that followed up the staircase. One of my chores was to dust these spindles every morning before going to breakfast which began at 7:00 a.m.

The head mistress and my father were standing together in the parlor. Like Pauline, Frank too was tall with a commanding presence and gait.

Good looking with dark auburn hair, his straight squared shoulders filled his dark suit perfectly. Unlike Pauline, he was of a gentle nature with a warm smile. My heart skipped a beat as I anticipated walking hand in hand with him to enjoy an ice cream cone. I couldn't remember when he had last visited me, but I was happy to see him, remembering a previous time when we walked hand in hand. I always felt safe with him. Our visits always felt too short, leaving me with sadness and an empty feeling when he left.

That moment of happy anticipation was shattered when one of the women who worked at the house appeared from the hallway with my suitcase in her hand. My heart dropped. I felt the overly familiar sense of suffocation as I choked back my high anxiety and tears. My fantasy of a visit with my dad enjoying a cool and delicious ice cream totally melted in the heat of an internal storm that raged within me. I liked it there and I did not want to leave. My mind raced with questions. Why did I have to leave? I had not done anything wrong.

With my suitcase in one hand and my hand in his other hand, Frank and I stepped onto the grand, covered front porch with white wicker furniture and hanging potted plants. We descended the wide painted staircase onto the tree-lined street. The leaves were starting to turn a golden color. I loved to swoosh through the pile of leaves just before the snow came. I didn't get to say goodbye to any of my playmates at the house. Did I go with my father to his home? Maybe. I don't remember.

"I, your priest, will make the whole earth my altar and on it will offer you all the labours and sufferings of the world." Hymn of the Universe Pierre Teilhard de Chardin

CHAPTER SIX

Flying Into the Storm

September 6, 1950. The TWA stewardess with a warm smile and eyes that danced with light in them, was very kind as she settled me into my seat in the front row of the airplane. She pinned the TWA wings on my sweater and patted me on my head declaring I was ready to take flight. The cabin was stifling. My father told me that my mother who was living in California had asked him to send me to her. I did not know that she was in California or where California was. I felt panic and deep sadness to be going to a strange place with a person I feared and, especially, to be leaving my father even though he wasn't in my life on a regular basis. I don't remember taking off from the airport nor the flight. I think I went to sleep instantly.

At the end of the flight, the stewardess woke me and personally escorted me off the airplane delivering me to Pauline. Pauline seemed a little warmer than usual and I could sense that she was happy to see me. This helped me relax a little as I wondered what was next.

Accompanying Pauline was a man named Bill who drove us to Pauline's little apartment on Lake Merritt in Oakland. The first memory I have is of the lake very near the apartment. It was adorned with a necklace reflecting amber-colored lights at night. Like magic the rippling water gave life to the amber necklace. I found this scene pretty and magically captivating. Fortunately, this scene turned out to be a haven for me as I spent many hours mesmerized by the magic of the dancing amber necklace.

Bill unloaded us at the front of a modest-sized apartment, leaving us standing there with my suitcase as he drove out of sight. Suitcase in hand, I followed Pauline to the entrance of the apartment building through a set of columns about four feet high, each with a large concrete ornamental lion on top as though guarding the apartment building.

The apartment was quite charming. For some unknown reason I felt a certain comfort once inside which was rare for me as I had learned to live on the sharp edge of the 'sword of survival' that was forever slaying the demons of intense fear and anger. Once inside the apartment I took in what seemed strangely abnormal for Pauline. She was calm and seemed genuinely pleased to have me there. The walls of the apartment contained a very tiny kitchen, a small but comfortable living room that opened through French doors into the bedroom and bathroom. I especially liked the double French doors with white shirred sheer curtains. The living room and kitchen window overlooked Lake Merritt.

A welcoming gift waiting for me was a small plastic doll with movable lashed blue eyes. She was dressed in a cute white with pink rosebuds crocheted dress and bonnet. Pauline had bought the doll for me. A lady who lived in the apartment below our apartment crocheted the dress and bonnet for Pauline. The lady who crocheted the dress and bonnet came to welcome me as well. A plump grandmother with a warm smile and gentle eyes, I found her to be comforting with the hope that she may be available if I needed an emergency escape from Pauline. I had not been able to bring any dolls with me from Pennsylvania, so this was a special and much needed surprise. I had learned to not put too much attachment to other people, however.

After the neighbor left, Pauline tucked me into the bed that we would share. She turned on the radio, she said, to keep me company while she would be away, telling me to not answer the door if anyone should knock. I don't know when she returned.

Pauline had registered me in a school in Oakland's Chinatown. I doubt she realized the school was in Chinatown. There were only three Caucasian girls in the school. No Caucasian boys. As far as I can remember this was my first exposure to Asians of any kind. What fascinated me most was that, after school, all the children fluttered like a school of fish to another building away from our school. Curious, I followed cautiously behind to see where they were going.

They were attending their mandatory Chinese school. I found myself fascinated by their calligraphy that was on the blackboard and the sing-song tempo of their language. Everything about the Chinese children, their beautiful faces, their sing-song language and their writing, especially, fascinated me.

Dying with curiosity to know more, I asked if I could come in and learn with them. Of course. NOT! The teacher closed the door to discourage me from hanging out at the threshold and disturbing the pupils in class. I waited outside for the Chinese children to complete their classes before they were allowed to come to the playground. There was no reason to hurry back to the apartment because it was always empty when I got there. I enjoyed the freedom of feeling alone and in charge of when I could choose to go home. It felt like it was my private home. Pauline's presence was not consistent at all. When I did come home, which always had to be before dark, to find Pauline there, I felt anxious and wished for her not to be there.

There was always some kind of food to eat, but cooked meals were not the norm. The one time I recall Pauline tried to broil some meat to have dinner together, she caught the pork chops on fire and almost set the kitchen on fire as she rushed the flaming pan to the sink to put running water on them. That was the end of dinner. Pauline quickly left. She clearly could not cope at all with what had taken place.

Breaking the reasonable calm since arriving, Pauline's real self finally emerged again like a demon.

I arrived home just before dark to find Pauline there. Instantly, fear overcame me. She was clearly angry and inebriated. Instantly I felt I was choking. Where had I been, she demanded. I told her I was playing in the school playground with friends from my class. Something set her off and she went into a tirade. She started screaming and throwing everything her eyes landed on. She ran from the kitchen to the living room like a possessed hurricane hurling anything and everything. She grabbed my doll and slammed it into the wall. The crocheted dress and bonnet held the broken pieces from scattering about. The doll's blue eyes just stared blankly from the floor. Pauline stormed out of the apartment slamming the door so hard the whole apartment shook.

Blinding light in my eyes and my volcanic stomach sent me into the bathroom to throw up after which I sought relief from the pain in my head by covering it with pillows under the covers on the bed.

Looking back, I believe Pauline really tried to settle down and be normal. Somewhere I got the story that Bill was a pilot who brought Pauline and, later, arranged for me to fly to Oakland from Pittsburgh, PA. She registered me in school with Bill's last name. This seemed strange. I thought perhaps she and Bill had gotten married and she was really going to be a sane and different person living a normal life.

I don't know if she changed her last name as well. He was never at the apartment after he had dropped us off the first night from the airport. Maybe Pauline went to his apartment for the night after I went to bed. If Bill had spent the night at our apartment one of us would have had to sleep on the couch because there was only one double size bed in one bedroom.

The only other memory of Bill is of me riding with him and Pauline around Oakland in his car. All the buildings we drove past were sadly gray and dingy just like the sky and my heart. There seemed to be no sunshine, no flowers or trees anywhere. It felt like a dead gray blob. I just wanted out of the car away from Bill and Pauline. I felt a suffocating heaviness with white hot tears that welled and fell from my eyes, blurring my vision.

Noticing the tears, Bill asked me what was wrong. The hot lump in my throat choked out any words I may have been able to speak. I didn't want Bill's attention. I just wanted to be out of there. I wanted to be alone. Looking back, I can imagine how stymied he may have been that I wasn't grateful for his efforts.

CHAPTER SEVEN

Continuing Journey of Unknowns

Not long after that Pauline and I were once again on a journey together like a vessel pushed from shore to the greater expanse of the sea of unknowingness. To where, I did not know. Cold silence chilled me to the bone.

With shallow breaths to not attract her attention, or wrath, I watched Pauline's reflection in the window of the Greyhound bus. As usual, I did not feel strong enough or brave enough to look at her directly.

Like a shadow, Pauline once again disappeared. She had deposited me with her brother and sister-in-law and their 3-year-old daughter in Healdsburg, CA. We lived in a cabin on the Russian River. The one-room cabin was made of shellacked knotty pine with a dank smell. My uncle and aunt slept in a double bed with my cousin tucked in with them. I slept crosswise across the foot of the bed cradled in a military canvas cot. We would all go to sleep listening to the radio playing soulful western and blues songs. My favorite was Johnnie Ray's "The Little White Cloud that Cried".

That winter the Russian river rose to ferociously devour the banks and the campground including our cabin. Gone was our home.

We then moved inland to a quonset hut. This was a two-bedroom box structure with a sheltered space that was used for storage and the homemade wine my uncle made. This was to be a temporary, summer placement.

Solace and friendship were to be found with a neighbor named Cara. She was tall, large boned with a big toothy smile and freckles galore. She exuded confidence, warmth and good humor. We immediately bonded into a close friendship. We slept on her family's screened-in summer porch to the sound of crickets' serenading on the hot summer nights.

Cara's family owned grape vineyards and a plum orchard in Geyserville. So that Cara and I could be together, her family gave me permission to join Cara in picking grapes and then plums on their ranch. We would be in the fields, ready to start picking fruit off the ground at sunrise. We and all the Mexican laborers who picked worked until noon when it became too hot to work. Lunch was served to all the pickers and staff at the ranch. After lunch, Cara and I would go to the Russian River and spend the afternoon together on the beach.

We were paid 0.25 cents per lug of fruit. There were easy picks such as the normal plums. The easiest were very large yellow plums that filled the lug quickly. The hardest were the French prunes which were very small and semi-dried. These had to be plucked from the crevices of huge dirt clods which must have resulted from rain that came after tilling the fields. A full day of picking the French prunes amounted to less than one-half bucket. Not a money maker at all. The money didn't really matter. I just wanted to be next to Cara and her family. Surprisingly, I earned $52.00 for the summer. My aunt said she would use that money to buy my school clothes in the fall. I left before fall or school arrived without my hard-earned cash. Cara and I became good pen pals until she suddenly stopped writing which hurt my feelings. Years later I learned that Cara had died in an auto accident. Like a branch that had been pruned from the tree of life, there was nothing left of Cara's and my friendship beyond a fond memory.

CHAPTER EIGHT

Call of the Siren

Heather and other friends and I were playing ball in the street in front of Heather's house which was not too far from where I was living in Oakland at the time. The distant sirens caused me to stop with an extremely uncomfortable feeling in the pit of my stomach. I quickly shook off the uneasiness and continued to play ball in the street. These strange feelings were familiar to me.

I returned home from Heather's house just before dark to see a fire truck at the bottom of the long steep driveway that led to the glass A-frame chalet where Marie and I lived. I recognized my smoldering day bed sitting outside. My skin crawled with cold, heart-stopping panic. Instantly I recognized the strange feeling that had overtaken me earlier when I heard the siren at Heather's house.

I remembered that I had come home from school to clean my white shoes. I was fanatical about my shoes always being white, not dirty. Also, I would not wear anything that was wrinkled. After I cleaned my shoes, I ironed a blouse before going out to play at Heather's house. The iron was a very heavy old-fashioned iron with only one setting. Hot. This was exactly like the one I had burned my hand on when I was living in the country of Pennsylvania. I had forgotten to unplug the iron. The cord was wrapped in fabric that got hot as the iron heated. I had placed the ironing board and iron next to my day bed in the corner of the great room of the tiny A-frame studio. Panicked, I ran back to Heather's house without continuing to my house. By now it was completely dark.

This house was one of my favorites. The A-frame chalet was made of total glass in the front. This is probably what saved the house and surrounding homes from burning down completely. I imagine that because the entire front of the chalet was glass, looming smoke was visible from the gas station below the driveway, causing someone to call the fire department.

At the top of the driveway was a tiny red brick patio at the entrance to the house shaded by and filled with a thicket of eucalyptus trees. The chalet was originally built as an artist studio. There was a very tiny bathroom to the right of the entrance, a small but utilitarian kitchen to the left. The great room was open with a couple of couches and a day bed. A ship's ladder led to the loft bedroom with a double-sized bed and one small dresser. This is where Marie slept.

Pauline had managed to find another place to drop me. Marie was an older woman who owned a restaurant in downtown Oakland. She did not have any children. She worked exceptionally long hours seven days a week which meant that unless I went to her restaurant, which was rare, I never saw her. On Saturday nights Marie would have a handful of friends over for a social gathering. To not be in the way of the adult party I was given money to take the Broadway Tunnel bus from downtown Oakland to Walnut Creek where I would stay with Marie's sister who had a daughter my age. Nancy and I became good friends. With anticipation of being with my friend and filled with a certain sense of airiness of freedom I looked forward to boarding the Broadway Tunnel bus in downtown Oakland each Saturday afternoon. We would go swimming at Walnut Creek High School and, at night, we would sneak out to climb into her tree fort near her house. Nancy's mother would make a delicious baked bean casserole. Full hot meals were a treat for me. Marie's sister would drive me back to the empty chalet on Sunday afternoon.

At the time of the fire, Marie had gone on vacation leaving me to live alone in her house. She told me that, for my safety, she had the gas turned off but that I had plenty of food in the refrigerator to eat that did not require cooking. My very favorite was grape jelly and butter on Wonder bread. Also, there were some potatoes which I liked to eat raw. I did not mind being alone at all as I was used to it and found it preferable to the noise and chaos that the alternative living situations seemed to usually offer, not to mention the shear fright of the viable alternative, being with Pauline.

During this time of 'camping' on my own in the chalet house that I loved, I was attending school for my third or fourth grade. During Marie's absence, I invited a friend from school to join me for dinner. Her parents agreed. They obviously did not confirm my situation. I was so excited to have a guest and proud to be sponsoring a dinner all by myself. I served extremely thin-sliced raw potatoes sprinkled with salt and pepper. So yummy, I thought. On the side were grape jelly sandwiches with milk.

The next day my guest/friend told me that when she got home after dinner and told her parents what we had, they fed her a 'real' meal and told her that she was not to play with me anymore. Sadness and shame filled my heart. Living in different foster homes, I got that rebuff a lot, but I couldn't get used to it enough that it didn't hurt my feelings. It was hard to understand because I knew I was a good person and had never done anything mean or bad to anyone.

After running quickly to Heather's house upon seeing the firetruck outside the chalet with my smoldering bed, Heather's mother called Marie's sister in Walnut Creek. I must have had her phone number for any emergency. Nancy's mother drove from Walnut Creek to Heather's to get me and take me back to stay with them for a while. Eventually, Nancy's mother took me back to the chalet and left me. Marie was still on vacation.

The burnt smoky smell was a painful reminder of what I had done. Neither Marie nor Pauline arrived for several days. I decided to sleep in

Marie's bed in the loft as it felt safer somehow. My other option was to sleep on one of the couches, but I felt open and vulnerable.

During the first night of sleeping at the chalet since the fire, I was awakened to the sound of a key being inserted in the door downstairs. I stayed frozen under the covers hoping I was safe in the loft. No lights were turned on. I heard the toilet downstairs flush. It was later that I learned Marie had an ex-husband who agreed to come stay in the middle of the night. I don't know when he began slipping into the house during the night. I never saw him. I only heard the key, the toilet flushing and some soft shuffling activity downstairs in the darkness.

Eventually Pauline arrived. Still alone, I had been sick in bed with a very high fever for what seemed like days. I don't remember ever again seeing Marie. I do not remember being taken from Marie's or where I went from there. There were intermittent stopovers at Pauline's apartments between homes so I can only assume this was one of those times.

Pauline's then-current boyfriend, Fred, was a soft-spoken and gentle man who tried to coordinate visits with the three of us by driving us around. Maybe he thought that was a way to keep Pauline present, if not focused.

Like a clever fox, Pauline would ask Fred to drop her off for a minute outside a bar saying that she had to go in to pay an outstanding bill. We watched her go in, expecting her to come back out in a few short minutes. Fred and I would wait in the car, double parked. Eventually, with no sign of Pauline, we would circle the block a few times expecting Pauline to finally be there on the curb waiting for us.

Eventually, Fred would park his car, leaving me in it while he would go into the bar. The bartender told Fred that Pauline came in one door and walked straight through and out the back door. This was a recurring theme. It was incomprehensible to me that Fred kept this farce going. Fred's eyes showed deep pain and confusion. He really cared about Pauline. I wanted to hug away his pain because I knew what he was feeling. Before driving me back home to drop me off, sans Pauline, Fred looked deep inside my eyes and held my shoulders. He tried to help me through the disappointing and painful situation. I knew it was really him he was trying to console.

Clearly, Fred had great expectations for himself and, especially, for Pauline. He had no way of knowing how seasoned I was in Pauline's and my relationship. He explained that my mother was extremely ill and needed hospitalization. He tried to explain to me that he was doing everything in his power to get her to a hospital. My heart ached for him as I knew Pauline all too well.

"Your pain is the breaking of the shell that encloses your understanding."
<u>The Prophet</u> Kahlil Gibran

CHAPTER NINE

Chaos Prevails

Like a magical leprechaun, Pauline seemed to appear and disappear with great agility, usually with a new man on her arm. Pauline and her latest victim, as I had come to call them, dropped me and his toddler son, Dennis, off for the night at the home of Alice and Mike. That was in June of 1952. Dennis' dad did return the next morning. When Alice asked where Pauline was, she was told that Pauline was nowhere to be found. Pauline had ditched her date the night before. ! Surprise!

There were several foster children of all ages living at Alice and Mike's house along with a couple of dogs and about 13 cats and kittens. Parents of these kids were seldom seen. The two front rooms were set up like dormitories with beds all along the walls. The center room was where we gathered to watch I Love Lucy, the Ed Sullivan Talent Show and The World of Disney. There was a built-in china cabinet with ceramic knick-knacks. The large dining table served as Alice's sewing center. Piles and piles of varied materials covered the top waiting to be made into girls' dresses, boys' shirts or curtains as needed. Alice's chair was surrounded by bushels and bushels of more material of all colors and patterns. Alice was obese, weighing about 360 pounds. She would sit at that table all day and well into the night smoking, eating potato chips and drinking Coca-Cola while sewing. She seemed obsessed with sewing new items with no regard for anything else that needed to be done in the house or with the little children left in her care.

A quiet man of few words, twinkling blue eyes and a resemblance to Spencer Tracy, Mike was 15-20 years older than Alice and of a much smaller stature. Mike was born into a proper Irish Bostonian family of teachers. For some reason he left home when he was 14. Although he didn't finish school he was well read and clearly intelligent. Having lived most of his adult life as one of the original boxcar hobos traveling across the country, Mike was a composite of many adventurous tales. Only occasionally would Mike share some of his adventures. In his youth, Mike clearly had a strong sense of adventure and the itchy feet to keep him moving along the long, lonely train tracks, stopping only long enough to earn a meal or a new pair of shoes. One of my favorite stories of Mike's was the time he hopped off the train in the middle of farm country in the Midwest. He approached a lonely-looking house in the middle of acres of land. He knocked on the door to see if there were any chores he could do for the owners in exchange for a meal and a night's rest. As it turned out, the husband was gone for a couple of days so help of any kind was greatly appreciated. A couple of nights later, he awoke to the sound of the old farm truck pulling up to the house. He quickly scrambled to get his clothes and shoes and once he heard the front door close, he managed to shimmy himself out of the second story window in the back of the house, hightailing it the "heck out of there" as he said. I tried to get him to record some of the stories as he had shared a few on occasion. With that twinkle in his blue eyes and little boy grin, he just laughed as he shook his head and said, "Oh NOOO, baby."

The thing I found most curious about Mike was that whenever he went out of the house, he ALWAYS wore his hat. Whether he was going to the store or walking the dog, he never went out without a hat. Always. I suppose it was a leftover DNA from his proper Bostonian roots. When he wasn't away at work Mike was either tending to his garden in the backyard where he grew green beans and tomatoes or cooking meals for the brood that had been deposited from many different places. Alice did not cook or clean. For these and many other reasons she was fast becoming my least favorite foster mother.

I, being the oldest, was told I would have to 'pay for my board' by helping around the house, because Pauline couldn't pay. That was an understatement. Mike and I did everything from washing and hanging diapers in the early morning air to housecleaning and cooking the meals for everyone. Although there was a constant change in the number of children who came and went, there were usually on average about three babies in diapers. The chaos and messiness of this house proved to be incredibly stressful for my sensitive psyche. I was constantly picking up toys and junk and trying to have a clean and organized space. There was no place to go for peace and quiet. I had to share my sleeping time with little ones who peed the bed. All the younger children cried often because they were stressed. Serenity did not know this place; its memo to stop by must have gotten swept away in a windstorm. The circumstances were jarring to my nerves after having been left alone for so many years. My debilitating headaches became increasingly frequent.

One bright-light exception was Bobby who lived there with his toddler sister. Bobby was a towhead, three years younger than I with a face speckled with freckles. We became very close, like brother and sister. He was by my side to help with the endless chores. He felt very protective of me when Alice would do or say mean or unkind things to or about me to the mothers who, on rare occasions, would come by to visit their children. Bobby was my saving grace. To this day I think of him with a loving and grateful heart. I hope his life has been well lived.

Together we made fun of all the chores we had to do. We would take hours to wash and dry the dishes because we would play around so much squirting each other with the baby bottle nipples or slipping the clean and dried dishes back into the sink with other dirty dishes. These shenanigans meant we had water all over the floor which meant we had to clean the floor as well. We didn't care because we were just happy to be together.

Although he was younger and smaller, I felt a certain comfort with him around. When we could find free time, we climbed all over the huge limbs of the cumquat tree in the backyard. We loved to pitch and hit softballs to each other in our large, fenced backyard that included the garden, the burning incinerator, and several large trees.

September. A new school year was beginning. I was entering sixth grade. Alice needed to register me in school but didn't have the necessary paperwork. No one knew where Pauline was (again). Somehow it all worked out as it always did in the past. I didn't see Pauline again until she arrived for the Thanksgiving holidays. In her usual manic way, she managed to totally upset the entire event and was asked to leave.

This was the longest and most turbulent time I had lived with any family. I did not like Alice, nor did I respect her for many reasons. Bobby, especially, and some of the other children who had come and gone made it all tolerable once I learned to accept the never-ending chaos and messiness, at least as much as I could. Loud noises, especially verbal confrontation, and mess threw me into an irritable and debilitating state of anxiety.

Mike would try to intervene and sneak little goodies to me and Bobby whenever he could without Allice knowing. Mike once managed to take us to Playland in San Francisco. This was not without a strong headbutt between Mike and Alice. Alice had come to depend on me for everything and clearly felt panicked at the thought of my not being there to do everything she wanted or needed to have done.

The other bright light of this chapter was my teacher, Herb Wong. He clearly was the most invigorating and interesting teacher I had ever had. He made everything fun and interesting. We learned about the Audubon Society by taking field trips, selecting a bird of choice and then creating a diorama of the bird in its environment with a summary of its characteristics. I chose the English Sparrow. Boring choice but I felt sorrow that no one wanted it because it was too ordinary and boring.

Herb Wong was a contributing writer for the Audubon books. After

I had my first child, he sent me copies of Audubon books that he had authored. He either liked me or felt sorry for me because he stayed in touch for years.

He taught us about jazz, particularly Dixieland jazz. He later became a late-night disc jockey for the Bay Area's jazz station, KJAZ. He wrote liner notes on the back of albums of famous jazz musicians.

Mr. Wong taught us about astronomy. We created personal 'telescopes' using the painted cylinder box of Quaker Oaks cereal. With a slit in one end, we could put the cardboard discs that we had made of a constellation pinpointed to view from the other end with an eye hole. He loved field trips. One trip was a nighttime field trip to the Chabot Observatory in Oakland where, he said, we could see sunshine at night. One by one each of us climbed on the step stool to peer through the giant telescope to see the sunshine at night. As each student stepped down, Mr. Wong whispered something in their ear. This brought snickers and a big smile to their faces. Sure enough, when looking through the telescope, SUNSHINE was as clear as day. SUNSHINE Biscuit Company, located in East Oakland.

Herb Wong is at the top of my list of favorite teachers. He went on to get his PhD at UC Berkeley after which he became Principal at the Washington Demonstration School in Berkeley where he met and married his wife. I was honored to be a guest at his wedding reception at the Empress of China in San Francisco's Chinatown in the late 1960's.

Rarely was I allowed to leave Alice and Mike's house with one wonderful exception. My best friend's parents would take Joan, her sister and me to the roller-skating rink every Friday night. Searching for that feeling of freedom was becoming like an addiction. I couldn't get enough. The overwhelming sense of freedom from being out of the house for any reason such as riding my bicycle extra, circuitous routes when going to the local corner grocery store or the butcher shop was intoxicating. Likewise, the heightened sense of freedom while gliding around the hardwood floor in my skates so swiftly creating a breeze in my hair. The euphoria of moving to the rhythm of the music, especially when the lights dimmed during couples' time. These were the things that always made my spirit soar like I was in a dream world of pure, unadulterated beauty. Added to that was the special comfort of my best friend, Joan, and her family who treated me like one of their own.

Feeling threatened by the lack of my presence to lean on, Alice would often find a reason to 'ground' me from the Friday night outings at the roller rink. Being a teen, feeling caged and rebellious, I defiantly walked out one Friday night and went to Joan's house with my roller skates even though Alice had told me I could not go skating that night. While skating I had no thoughts of regret or worry of what consequences would be awaiting me once I got home from skating.

When I arrived home, the atmosphere was as dark and heavy as a fast-approaching storm. To my disappointment, Mike was 'on Alice's side'. Feeling enraged with anger, I mouthed off to them with fury. Both Alice and Mike looked stunned. Absolute silence filled the air for what seemed like eternity. All the other kids froze in silence. Mike turned abruptly, left the room and quickly returned with his leather razor strap. I was shocked that he, who was always so gentle and soft spoken, could be so violent. A vivid flashback rushed in of that one fateful day when daddy wielded his razor strap haphazardly all over my body. This time, however, I fought back, trying to grab the strap from Mike's hands. Alice just backed off and watched. I had to be kept home from school for a week until the bruises were faded enough to be covered with makeup.

Quite surprisingly, Pauline did arrive for my sixth-grade graduation. Although she was dressed nicely and she did manage to not make a scene, I was humiliated by her obvious drunkenness, her wobbly gate and breath that smelled of bourbon. It ruined my day, and I couldn't wait to go home and for her to leave.

The only other time I remember Pauline visiting me during the few years I lived with Alice and Mike was during Christmas. I do not remember what year it was. Alice and Mike were far from affluent, but they did the best they could for all of us as most of the parents, except Bobby's, were absent. We each got to have one request for a Christmas present. Music was my solace and escape. I asked for a radio. A beautifully wrapped little aqua-colored radio was waiting for me under the tree that Christmas morning. My heart felt like it was going to burst with joy and gratitude to have something so precious of my very own ability to escape into music.

Pauline was invited to join us later that day for Christmas dinner. As usual, she became quite drunk and went into her usual schizoid-maniac tirade. Pauline was escorted out the door. On the way she picked up my radio and hurled it across the room into the wall. The rest of my day was spent in the comfort of one of the beds in the front room after throwing up in the bathroom. The smell of food was nauseating to me.

Pauline eventually moved from Oakland to Santa Cruz. By now I was attending Roosevelt Junior High School in Oakland. Mike would escort me by bus to downtown Oakland to put me on the Greyhound bus to Santa Cruz where Pauline lived with her then-current boyfriend.

Once the early morning fog lifted around 11:00 a.m., Pauline and I would walk from her summer cabin to the boardwalk. Pauline would plant me on a patch of sand, give me a couple of quarters and proceed across the street to a little bar. Once again, I loved the freedom of being alone. I loved the sun and saltwater as I was tossed and slammed while body surfing. In the late afternoon, early evening, as the beach became empty and the sun was slipping into the sea, Pauline could be seen weaving across the sand like a sidewinder. Together we would walk back to the cabin. As much as I was terrified and disgusted to be walking with her, I tried to steady her to keep her walking in a straight line. Although I did not know anyone there, I felt deeply ashamed and embarrassed to be seen with Pauline. She was usually too inebriated to cook and would go straight to bed. Her boyfriend had disappeared right after I arrived. I found whatever I could to eat.

Surprisingly, Pauline managed to not blow a fuse on any of these few times I visited her in Santa Cruz. More surprisingly, I enjoyed being in Santa Cruz. The warm sand of the beach, tumbling in the surf, the sounds of the rickety wooden rollercoaster and screams from the children at the beach were fun. As the time to go back to Mike and Alice neared, I felt a heavy cloud of dread and anxiety. Which of these two worlds brought me the greatest anxiety?

What seemed like an exceptionally long bus ride back to Oakland was only two hours, but it felt timeless as I wished the ride would never end.

To my relief, Pauline did not appear for my junior high school graduation. I felt free to enjoy my day and my friends for this exciting event. Surprisingly, I was thankful to see Alice had arrived for graduation. Maybe because I was proud to be one of the speakers. Even though I did not like or respect her, it felt good to have someone there for this event just like all the other children graduating. Despite all the chaos and changes throughout my childhood I was always a good student and have always loved reading, music and learning new things. I had long ago found that my favorite place away from home was in the library which I found to be noticeably quiet and full of interesting information.

"This human shape is a ghost made of distraction and pain. Sometimes pure light, sometimes cruel, trying wildly to open, this image tightly held within itself." The Illuminated Rumi Translations & Commentary by Coleman Barks

CHAPTER TEN

Psycho Ward

Tenth grade. It had been several years, though it felt like many lifetimes, since I had felt the experience of escaping into 'other worldliness' where I floated in luminous energetic fields of undulating colors graced with light beings. There started to appear a tunnel with a light at the end. I found myself measuring time with anticipation of escaping to something better, something higher. Is this not so for all teens? However, a certain heaviness seemed to again be slowly creeping in, threatening to suffocate me.

Pauline had moved back to Oakland. I was a fully budded young lady who could no longer live with Alice and Mike as the temptation was too overpowering for Mike. The only alternative was to live with Pauline again.

As before, we shared a double-sized murphy bed that took up all the space in the living room leaving only inches between the foot of the bed and the couch. The kitchen had a small cream-colored ceramic wood burning stove with two burners and a well to put wood in for heat, a small drop table with two chairs and a pull-down ironing board which I liked because I was still anal about not wearing wrinkled clothes.

Night after night strange noises awoke me. Pauline was being escorted home and poured into bed by a stranger, or two, after the bar closed. I hated sleeping with her and bristled whenever her hand or body touched mine. I felt like I was trapped, choking and dying a very slow death with no oxygen to breathe, no place to escape.

Years earlier while exploring the library, I noticed several rows of large yellow telephone books. The books were from all over the United States. As I had done several times before I again looked in the directory to find my father's name in the Pittsburgh, PA directory. He was still listed. This amazed me because, after the many previous times when I wrote and tried to convince him that I needed him and a home in which he repeatedly rejected my plea, I fully expected that he would have changed his listing to an unpublished phone number and address. On one of the earlier writings to him he wrote back telling me that he was remarried and had two sons. He asked me to please not write to him again. However, desperation led me to attempt to get him to change his mind every few years until he finally just ignored my letters. His parents were also listed in the phone directory. I once called them collect. His mother answered and suggested I not call again or write to them or my father.

Regardless of her age, Pauline's drinking, smoking and general lifestyle had robbed her of her natural beauty. She looked incredibly old. Her body was that of a skeleton except for her puffy face and ever-expanding distended stomach. Her behavior was becoming more manic and violent. The few times we were together in the apartment she would consistently go into a violent outburst where anything and everything, including sharp kitchen knives, were hurled against the walls and at me. One time the adjacent neighbor came to the door demanding that we keep the noise down because his pregnant wife was getting extremely upset. He further went on to say that he would have to call the cops if the noise and disruption did not stop. I was hoping he would call the cops because I would have considered that my voice could be heard, and it could be my rescue from there.

Just as I had when I was six years old, I found myself being awakened by the heavy air of a threatening presence. Pauline, reeking of booze, was over my body with one of her skinny pants belts tethered at each end by each of her hands, putting the belt around my neck. Powered by the adrenalin of the fright and flight syndrome, my arms and feet came up upon her, sending her falling backwards against the foot of the bed. I grabbed my purse and whatever clothes were on the dresser, running out of her apartment.

I called a friend of Alice and Mike who had boarded at their house briefly while he was getting established in his relocation from another state. Martin told me I could come to his apartment. He lived quite a distance from Pauline's apartment but, somehow, I got there in the dark of night, running all the way. Shortly after I got into his apartment, two police cars pulled up. They took him aside to talk. They took me aside and asked me what was going on. I told them the history of Pauline and me and, specifically, what had just happened. I told them that I would not, under any circumstances, go back to Pauline's apartment. They said I had to go back, offering to drive me. They said they would talk with her. When I told them I was not going to stay they said I would then be picked up and forced to live in the juvenile cottages that were run by the county. I told them that sounded like a wonderful option.

They did drive me back to Pauline's to have a talk with her. Looking back, I am amazed that they allowed me to be with Pauline who was a clear threat to my life. I don't remember. All I remember is feeling numb with fear.

One Sunday, Alice and Mike's friend, Martin, checked in to see how things were going. As usual Pauline was not around. I asked him to take me for a ride to someplace with many trees. The need to feel connected with nature like I did when I lived in the country of Pennsylvania was overwhelming.

Martin drove up a winding road to the top of the Oakland hills. The aroma of eucalyptus was transcendent. Martin parked so I could get out, view the breathtaking panorama of the Bay below, feel the silvery leaves and breathe deeply the powerful aroma of the eucalyptus buds. It was all so wonderfully therapeutic.

Quietly, he sat in the car watching me. I felt safe with him. When it came time for him to drive me back to Pauline's apartment, hot salty tears streamed down my cheeks; tears of gratitude for communing so deeply with nature and tears of sadness to not be able to just sit there forever. Despite the tears, the lovely aroma of the trees and the peaceful feel of nature helped alleviate the heavy feelings of sadness and fear to a certain extent.

Martin cautiously made himself more available to me as a safety net. Like a drug, all I wanted was the wonderful smell and heavenly feeling of being among the eucalyptus high above the city. I told Martin that I would give anything to live among those trees.

Like a pinprick into an air-filled balloon Martin announced that he loved me, wanted to marry me and give me a home among the trees once I became of age. Martin was thirteen years older than I.

Instantly, I felt threatened and devastated. Once again, I felt I was suffocating. Why did he have to ruin everything? I just wanted peace, quiet and the solace of the trees. Selfishly, I did not care to be with him at all, but he was the means for my getting to the trees. I was too frozen with fear to say anything except that I needed to go back to Pauline's apartment. Apparently, Martin got in touch with Pauline to confess his love for me and ask her permission to marry me when I turn sixteen, which was less than a year off. My God! Clearly, he did not know Pauline or he would never have put me in such jeopardy. Pauline came totally unglued at the knowledge I had been slipping around with a man thirteen years older than I. I had to escape. I ran to the corner phone booth and called the number on the card that the policeman had given me, saying I desperately needed a home immediately. The person on the other end of the line told me that I would have an interview appointment with a social worker as soon as possible. That was not soon enough as far as I was concerned. I needed someone now. Silence. By the time I walked around town for awhile and got back to the apartment, Pauline was gone.

The next day at school I told my friend, Lenny, that I would be leaving

Oakland High soon but did not know where I would be going. I gave him some of the details, making him promise not to tell anybody. He promised he would not discuss my situation with anyone.

"You are what your deep, driving desire is. As your desire is, so is your will. As your will is, so is your deed. As your deed is, so is your destiny." (Brihadaranyaka Iv.4.5) The Upanishads Introduced & Translated

CHAPTER ELEVEN

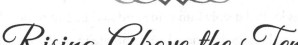

Rising Above the Tempest

By now I was aware of what others referred to as my daydreaming. It was becoming clear that, in some unknown way, through daydreaming, I could somehow take charge of my life. I did not know how, but I knew deep down there was some untapped reservoir of power. Having discovered the hills with the wonderfully aromatic trees did something inside me. It was like letting the genie out of the lamp and the tiny bird finding that his outstretched wings gave him flight. I instinctively knew that, somehow, I could manifest the eucalyptus trees around me.

I do not remember the exact genesis of the next chapter of my journey. I remember meeting a wonderful mature woman who was tiny with a very distinct crooked nose and sparkling blue eyes. Her wispy sandy-grey colored hair was tied in a bun on top of her head. Her bright red lips were in a perpetual smile. I still feel warmth when I think of Dr. Janet MacCleod. My guess is that she came to school and met me in my high school counselor's office. Although I really do not remember, I assume she asked many questions. Desperate to escape from Pauline I openly and honestly shared what was taking place in my private life with high anticipation that at last I was going to be able to make a final escape to safety before my sixteenth birthday.

Dr. MacCleod was the head psychologist for the Oakland School District. My favorite high school teacher, Mrs. Betty Wilson, had contacted Dr. MacCleod after my friend Lenny told her about me and my situation.

Mrs. Wilson was my Civics teacher. She was also the school's 'Mother Theresa' whom all the students admired and to whom they could go for counseling and guidance. She was truly exceptional as a person as well as a teacher.

When I confronted Lenny for having broken his promise, his huge warm brown eyes looked deeply into mine and said he had to do whatever he could to help me because he knew I was not safe in my living situation. He said that he had discussed my situation with his parents to see if I could live with them. His parents told him that he needed to be my voice at school and tell an authority there although he had promised me he would not tell anyone.

Lenny was like the school's Big Brother with a huge heart for anyone needing a warm hand. His concern was so obvious and genuine I could not be angry with him. In fact, I was starting to feel relief and even anticipation of what might follow. A gentle stirring in my heart felt comforting. This was something I had not felt for years and years, not since the very brief visit with Aunt Helen and cousin Bill.

"The force that created the unimaginable splendors and the unimaginable horrors has taken refuge in us, and it will follow our commands." St. Catherine of Siena

CHAPTER TWELVE

Gateway Opens

During the interim of Dr. MacLeod and Mrs. Wilson working together to find a home for me, Dr. MacLeod arranged and paid for me to attend a camp in Northern California. I do not know exactly where this camp was. It was a long bus ride to finally arrive in a thick forest of tall redwood trees whose fragrance was equally as heady as the eucalyptus trees.

Feeling a certain exhilaration around freedom from commands and endless domestic duties sparked within me the idea that maybe, just maybe, there were greater things out there for me to discover. I wondered if my daydreaming had anything to do with this new stirring of realization.

The camp experience was enriching and fun with swimming in the river as well as various crafts and projects. Best of all was absolute freedom from anyone or anything else outside of the camp. I did not think of anyone, nor did I miss anyone back home. I was totally living in the here and now of the moment. Best was the aroma of tall trees.

The highlight and wrap-up of the camp session was acting in the play, Pandora's Box. I was chosen to play the role of Pandora. The stage was the dirt floor except for an elevated spot at the base of a huge redwood tree. Somehow there were portable lights set upon the stage area. Nervously excited to be 'shining' while standing against the large tree with blinding lights, I gave a stellar performance in my makeshift costume of white, enjoying every minute of it. That is, until I became stage fright and froze in the middle of a line. I could hear whispers of the lines coming at me, but I was too numb with fear to decipher what the words were. It happens to the best of actors, the counselors reassured me. Their kindness did not stop me from feeling embarrassed and ashamed. I felt I had ruined it for everyone; that another person would not have miscarried the play that way.

During the time I was at camp Mrs. Wilson contacted her best friend, Jane and husband, Peter, who had taken in one other foster child in the past as well. Being benevolent people, they had also sponsored two refugee families from Hungary and one refugee family from Germany.

Jane and Peter explained to Mrs. Wilson that they were not interested in sponsoring any more foster children and that they were just on their way to vacation in Mexico. Vouching for my character and desperate circumstances, Mrs. Wilson asked them to think about it while on vacation and to please agree to have one meeting with me and Dr. MacCleod.

Some people are incredibly golden. Their memory forever lingers with the ones whose lives they have touched. Such was the essence of Dr. MacCleod who, even in this writing, fills my heart with deep gratitude and joy for having been blessed by her presence in my life. She was known for her very compassionate actions toward less fortunate children throughout the Oakland school system. She generously gave of her time, invited us to her home and was always there as needed.

A couple of weeks after returning from camp, Dr. MacCleod picked me up in front of Pauline's apartment to drive me to meet a family that she thought would be very good for me and that I might like, especially since they had a daughter my age and a son three years younger. Trepidation and anticipation swirled within.

Before we stepped through the front door, Jane met us. A beautiful tiny woman with large green eyes, wearing a simple short-sleeved top and flowing skirt awash with petite flowers greeted us. Her very gracious smile felt like a tremendous hug from the universe. With an air of Asian elegance, Jane bowed her head slightly as her outstretched hands guided me over the threshold. Was I dreaming? Never had I met anyone like this. Never had I been received so lovingly – with the one exception of my aunt and cousin on that extremely brief visit to Scranton, Pennsylvania when I was a toddler!

After entering the house, I was instantly shocked and panicked to see Pauline sitting on the sofa. My initial thought was that she was there to terrorize me and the situation. I immediately felt trapped, panicked and betrayed by Dr. MacCleod that she hadn't told me Pauline would be there as well. Dr. MacCleod explained that Pauline had been invited, she explained to us all, to be a part of the visit because if this family agreed to take me into their home and care for me, they would expect to have legal guardianship, which needed Pauline's approval. The only question Pauline asked was how much it would cost her for me to stay with them. I was told at Alice and Mike's that I had to work for my room and board, which I did.

Once it was explained by Dr. MacCleod that by giving Jane and Peter full guardianship and, possibly adopting me, Pauline would have no further obligation to me as her parent. Pauline gave her permission without a second thought and quickly departed in a cab. Pauline seemed as panicked about getting away from there as I felt panicked at seeing her there. Dr. MacCleod and I visited with the family to get acquainted. Once I heard the door of the cab close, I felt I could breathe again.

Jane explained that her husband, Peter, should be home any minute. At that moment their daughter, Ann, appeared from another room. Tall and bronze-tanned with a beautiful bigger-than-life white toothy smile, sparkling dark eyes that seemed to beg for the drama of something mischievous, Ann's powerful raw presence filled the room as she slinked through slowly like a svelte panther, evaluating me and the situation.

Like an active movie silenced on the pause mode, Ann clearly held a presence that was commanding. During this one brief frozen timeframe, Ann took all the oxygen out of the room. Intimidation, wonder, awe and curiosity drew me to her. She was someone totally at the other end of the spectrum from myself or my life; a spectrum I never knew existed. I wanted to know more about Ann's intoxicating mystique. Something inside me clicked at the intuitive prospect of greater expanses and potentialities for me, for my life, that clearly lay mysteriously far beyond what I had ever known or imagined. Regardless of my numerous other-world-dream experiences this was real, down to earth. This was honest to God real, not the airy-fairy experiences I had had.

Suddenly Ann's magic spell was broken, and the group animation continued as the front door burst open with the force of a hurricane. A tall, dark-skinned handsome man with a white toothy smile like Ann's and a familiar spark of liveliness in his dark brown eyes announced boldly "I am here!". We could see that. His arms were outstretched as though to embrace the whole world. There was no question that Ann was her father's daughter. As though there was no room now for both dynamos, Ann slipped away quietly to another room.

Ever the consummate gentle mother, Jane put her arms around my shoulders as though protecting me while introducing me and Dr. MacCleod to Peter. I remember so clearly a very strange sensation that overcame me. It was like I was fading away, unable to grab on or stay grounded. My head shook a second of its own volition. I KNEW this person. From where I had no idea. Looking into the warm pools of his smiling eyes was like looking into a portal of an ancient time and place. It had been years since I had experienced otherworldliness like this. There was no doubt in my heart that this was going to be my next home and family.

I left their home on the hill feeling the aliveness of love in my heart for the beautiful grace and gentleness of these people. Most unbelievably, their house was among the very same fragrant eucalyptus trees above Skyline Blvd. overlooking the City of Oakland where Martin had brought me on those Sunday escape drives and where I announced to him that THIS is where I wanted to live, amongst the heady scent of the eucalyptus trees.

After our meeting with Jane and Peter at their home above Skyline Boulevard, Dr. MacCleod returned me to the dismal studio apartment with the murphy bed that Pauline and I shared.

Dr. MacCleod's forever sparkling eyes and perpetual smiling lips were entrancing. How does one speak with a continual smile on their lips, I wondered. On the drive home, she asked me what I thought, what was I feeling? Too stunned with fear of so much unknown while, simultaneously, transfixed on what I knew was to be the next chapter, living among the fragrant eucalyptus, living in a clean, orderly home with pleasant and polite people, I swallowed hard and downplayed the hurricane of wild feelings with a one-word response in a very soft voice. "Nice", I said.

Dr. MacCleod continued talking as she drove, espousing a litany of 'what ifs'. "IF I should be accepted into this family ....and, IF this should happen to 'turn sour'. On and on she went with many 'what ifs', all the while with that perpetual smile.

It was all too overwhelming for me to comprehend and maintain my equilibrium. I felt numb. I felt terrified at going back to Pauline's apartment for fear she may lash out at me in one of her violent tirades at the situation. My stomach began to churn, the light began to blind my eyes and her voice became painfully magnified in my ears.

Once I left Dr. MacCleod's car, I quickly made it to the bathroom in the apartment.

While Dr. MacCleod waited to hear confirmation of whether Jane and Peter had agreed to accept me as their foster child, it was arranged that I would temporarily go back to Alice and Mike's house. It was clear that staying with Pauline was neither wise nor safe. Alice was happy with this as she never wanted me to leave in the first place. My intuition told me I would not be at Alice and Mike's for long. All I could think about was the home on the hill among the eucalyptus and the wonderful people who lived there. Over and over in my mind I relived my experience there.

The next memory was that of Peter arriving in his beige convertible VW bug to pick me up from Alice and Mike's house, the little shanty situated in an alley. Alice, Mike, a couple of toddlers and I had moved to this house from the bigger one a few miles away. At the current house there were only a few of us as it was a tiny one bedroom with an add-on space. Alice slept on the sofa downstairs. I and the few younger children shared the one bedroom upstairs. Mike slept in the very narrow added-on room adjacent to where we children slept.

When we were living in the other, bigger house I had returned from school one day to find Alice upset that they had been given notice to move because the house we were in was going to be torn down for an apartment building. Having moved all my life, I did not understand why moving was so upsetting. I suggested they buy their own house so they would not be forced to move as renters; they could be there forever, if they chose. They said they could not possibly afford to buy a home.

Determined, why I am not sure, I began to search for a house they could buy. In those days there was not a constant sea of professional For Sale signs on houses. People didn't move that often. Not finding any For Sale signs on any houses along the main streets that I usually walked to and from school, I had a thought to walk through tucked-in alleyways.

Eventually I came across a little house situated above the alleyway on a slight slope with a one-car garage built into the hillside. It had a generic red and white FOR SALE sign nailed to the front of the house with a phone number written on it. I wrote down the phone number and took it home to Alice and Mike. They continued to tune me out saying that they could not afford to buy a house. I insisted they did not know unless they tried, suggesting they at least call the phone number.

They moved into their very own first and only home a few months later. The purchase was made possible because the seller carried the financing.

During the interim time that we were waiting to see if the Jane and Peter had decided to accept me into their home, and after returning from the summer camp that Dr. MacCleod had treated me to, Alice and Mike were told that I would be with them only temporarily for a very brief time because I would be leaving them to go to another home.

CHAPTER THIRTEEN

Sparrow Takes Flight

On September 5th, 1958, Peter picked me up from the little lopsided shanty with a white picket fence situated on the slope above the alley. I do not remember if Mike was there. Alice cried and hugged me. While I felt uncomfortable and sad for Alice, I could not wait to escape their home and the circumstances that caused me to have to leave and live with Pauline in the first place. In retrospect I realize that Alice was not really a mean person. She was just very lazy. In my childish logic and opinion, she had no business taking in foster children because she was not willing or able to really care for them. Mike, I and any other older resident child who could take care of the younger ones would cook and do laundry as directed by Alice. I was told more than once that my mother could not afford to pay so I had to work for my room and board.

This meant getting up extra early to cook breakfast to feed all the younger kids, including at least one or two babies. The regime included washing diapers and hanging them out to dry and be taken down and folded at the end of day before helping Mike cook dinner.

It was the day before my 16th birthday. Peter loaded my two paper bags of clothes into the car. To my amazement, Peter drove up the familiar road to the beautiful landscape of eucalyptus trees along the serpentine Skyline Boulevard that majestically overlooked the City on the Bay. I could not believe my eyes; surely this was not really happening.

For the first time I felt trepidation at the thought of change. Change of homes had always been an exciting expectation because I always imagined something better to move toward. What I felt with Jane and Peter was unlike anything I had ever felt before.

Excited and nervously anxious, the voice of Dr. MacCleod played over and over in my mind; "IF this should turn sour" she had repeated often. What did she mean by 'sour'? I often reflected, or rather worried, more than I reflected trying to anticipate what that meant. What would I do and where could I possibly go next if this turned "sour"? Clearly, Pauline had never been a significant part of my life, at least not in any positive way. I had no other connections or places for me to go that seemed even remotely feasible. The aunts that I knew very briefly as a very young child were non-existent. If they were in touch with Pauline, I have not been aware.

I remember staying with many other people for very brief times including a wonderful big black lady with whom I felt safe, but there was no real memory or connection of anyone that I could turn to at this time.

Just as I had found Frank listed in the phone book that was in the local library, so too were his parents, my grandparents. Recalling how I had called them collect when I found myself back at Pauline's for that brief respite while waiting to go to the new home only to be rejected by them caused me to once again feel like I was suffocating They had already told me to not call again, but I felt I had to. They were coolly cordial. However, they said that my return to them or Frank was not a possibility. Strangely, they sent me a bracelet after that one call. The only gift or word I got from them. The door of any other option of going back to Alice and Mike's house had been permanently closed.

I felt relieved to close the door on my life thus far and especially from Alice and Mike's house. I called Martin to tell him my news and that I would not be seeing him anymore. His voice became broken as he reminded me that I had said I would give ANYTHING to live among those trees. It seems, he said, that I had even given away his love and desire to give me the house of my dreams. My heart sank for him as I fought back the hot tears. The phone went dead. No goodbyes. I did feel sorry for Martin and was grateful for the little escapes he offered by driving me to the trees, but I didn't expect such a sharp cut in the relationship. Like awakening from a dream, Martin was permanently gone from my life just as so many other people with whom I had walked.

Stunned by the sudden silence of the phone and the sense of a heavy wall that seemed to drop in front of me I was beginning to feel I was living on a conveyer belt, passing by a myriad of scenes in which I was an actor stepping off and on, changing costumes and identity like a chameleon or shaman shapeshifter. My life did not feel real at all, whatever that feeling was supposed to be. Feeling as light as a feather carried by the wind, I felt overwhelmingly disconnected from what was supposed to be so-called normal. I was beginning to feel heavy and tired despite my anticipation of the next new chapter among the eucalyptus trees.

A few years later Alice called to tell me that Martin had died in a fatal car crash while driving under the influence of alcohol.

September 6th. My birthday. A new day, A new chapter. This was the first experience of awakening in a new bedroom and home. The room was spacious, the bed comfortable. I especially liked the window that had wooden mini shutters that covered half-way up the windows. Over the tops of the shutters, I could lie in bed and see the swaying leaves of the eucalyptus trees. The clean quiet was deeply welcome and nurturing.

That afternoon I was astonished to see that Jane and Peter knew it was my birthday. I had not told them. Not a big celebratory event, it was sweetly understated, much more than I had usually received in the past. Growing up feeling invisible it was not uncommon to have no mention of my birthday. Never from Frank and very rarely from Pauline. I felt humbled and special all at once.

The gifts I received included a beautiful fountain pen from Chief, the German Shepherd. After opening the gift from Chief, a large white box with a simple pink ribbon and bow was presented. It felt strangely light, as though it was empty. My first thought was that it was a joke gift, just an empty box. As it turned out there was nothing in the box. However, taped to the underside of the box lid was a small envelope that contained two tickets to see the movie Porgy & Bess.

An additional birthday surprise was that Lenny's mother and Lenny arrived for me and drove Lenny and me, cramped into her racy red 190 SL Mercedes, to the Lake Merritt area where Lenny and I were dropped off for dinner before seeing the movie, Porgy & Bess. My maiden date at sweet sixteen. Warm. Memorable. Porgy & Bess will always be a favorite of mine, especially the song, Summertime.

Lenny was rightfully bursting with pride that he was the main instigator in creating a positive change for me and my life. He wanted me to have something tangible to remember him, my sixteenth birthday and the kickoff of a new chapter. He presented me with an elongated jade pendant. I later had the pendant made into a ring because the pendant kept falling out of its clasp. I still have this ring. This was clearly a fabulous celebration of a new chapter that was absolutely like no other experience in my life so far. Gratitude filled me completely. For once I felt like I was breathing, that the oxygen was not completely blocked and out of reach because of fear and anxiety.

Tickets to see Porgy & Bess were the introduction to an entirely new panorama of life for me. Over the many years Jane enjoyed sharing certain authors, poetry and Broadway with me. I felt like a sponge that could not soak up enough of the beauty of this new world. She took me to see my first play in New York, Pygmalion, and on two other occasions to see the West Side Story and Music Man. Together we enjoyed art galleries, art exhibits and foreign films. Life was bountiful beyond my greatest expectations. Gratitude filled my heart.

"All this is full. All that is full. From fullness, fullness comes. When fullness is taken from fullness, fullness still remains." Upanishads Translated. By E. Easwaran

CHAPTER FOURTEEN

Nesting Safely Among the Trees

Natural beauty, tranquility and warm loving people filled this home and my heart. Something for which my soul had been desperately thirsting from as far back as I could remember. I just wanted to sit and take it all in. No more being rushed into endless chores, trying to maintain a clean and orderly home, no more being manipulated to serve others' less than honorable needs, no longer having to share a sofa sleeper with a bed-wetter.

I could come home to peace and quiet in my own space to do homework which I loved. Feeling like I had been transported to another world, I was grateful for the peace, serenity, and orderliness.

Two of my favorite parts of the house included the bay window of the living room that framed a thicket of trees. Situated in front of this scene was a very low, antique black with red flowers and birds lacquered oriental table. On top sat a beautiful rice paper lamp with dried flowers and butterflies embedded in the rice paper. Lovely ambiance with the soft luminous light when lit was especially beautiful.

At the front entry was a pony wall with the same stone that was on the fireplace framed with two heavy wooden shelves. Situated on the shelves were two or three huge, antique books. I wanted very much to look through them, but I was afraid the pages may crumble from age. I never saw anyone open them and I was not invited to open them.

Sitting majestically on one of the shelves was a large, concrete statue of Quan Yin. At the time I did not know who Quan Yin was, but I was transfixed with her just as I had been when I once passed a doorway in Oakland's Chinatown as an eight-year-old. At that time, the strange sound of Buddhist monks chanting drew me to the doorway from where the sounds floated. I felt myself warmly bathed in the strange sounds. Something about the Quan Yin statue evoked those same feelings. I still live with Quan Yin, the Chinese table and the rice paper lamp which Jane gifted to me over the years. Omnipresent is a deep subtle connection to the soul-soothing feelings and memories as the energy of Jane's regal essence continues to fill our home through these lovely gifts. By divine grace I was guided to a true, loving mother.

Beautiful were the warm tones of the buff-colored Arizona flagstone floor-to-ceiling fireplace. It had an extended hearth at sitting height. We would sit and listen to music with the fire blazing. When Peter's sister, Paulette, visited, she would sit on the hearth to play the guitar and sing folk songs.

It felt safe to breathe and relax. Here, I no longer felt invisible. I was included in the everyday conversations. My thoughts and feelings were invited and accepted. Personal choices were honored. I could commune with nature by walking alone on nearby paths and sleeping in a sleeping bag on the ground outside the house enveloped by the fragrance of eucalyptus.

To my dismay, however, I began to experience a current of unsettling anxiety that often brought unexpected tears for no apparent reason. It did not make any sense to me because I felt at peace and very content to be in the home and presence of Jane and Peter. Having come from a life of survival, I seemed to know enough to hide the anxiety for fear I would not be allowed to stay.

My hopes of forging a close relationship with young siblings, Ann and Michael, were dashed as Ann was sent to private school in Ojai, Southern California, one week after I had arrived. She did not stay there long. Her parents thought Ann would love the small campus atmosphere with horses to ride. It was too confining for Ann's free-spirited nature. When she returned from the private school, she announced that she wanted to leave home to be totally independent, free of rules. High spirited as the animals in the wild, she left home almost immediately for an early and brief marriage. We knew, as did Ann, I'm certain, that the marriage to the young boy not far from home was only an interim ticket to complete freedom. As expected, that marriage did not last long at all. Leaving the marriage and the extended family who all lived under the same roof, she was able to fling open the doors to live her life on her terms.

Beautifully flashing, bold, colorful and primal, Ann created many, many poignant chapters in her life. Her one solid, but also brief relationship was with the marriage to the father of her wonderful son. Ann's heart was as big as her eyes and flashing smile. She would give the blouse off her back, her shoes and her last dime to a homeless person. She had a genuine compassion for the down and trodden. Ann played with the many men who were drawn to her as a moth to the flame, as a cat plays with a moving toy mouse.

Eventually, it became evident that Ann suffered deeply from the effects of bipolar disease throughout her adult life. My heart always felt deeply for her. At the same time, I also felt guilty that perhaps I had contributed to her illness, or, at least that I shouldn't have the warmth and kind attention of her parents as she may have felt replaced.

Michael, who was a young teenager in junior high when I arrived expressed no interest in another sibling relationship. In the second year Michael too was sent to a boarding-prep school and then to college. Like fine wine, special relationships did evolve with Ann and Michael over our adult years. Ann and I enjoyed getting together when her son and my daughter were young toddlers. I, Michael and his lovely wife, Karen, have maintained a warm familial relationship to this day.

Early in my thirties when I began to search ways to buy a home for myself and my children, Michael very kindly approached me and offered to help me buy my first home, a two-bedroom condo in San Jose. We entered into a written agreement. Two years later when I sold the condo for another larger home, he graciously passed on taking any profit or interest on the money he loaned, which was most of the down payment. Thanks to Michael and his generous seed capital, I enjoyed several homes from which the condo was a springboard. I do not know if I could have enjoyed the many homes that followed without his help initially. These are the types of acts or actions that are never discussed between Michael and me but are never forgotten and sit in my heart's pool of gratitude.

In retrospect, it is my guess that the idea of sponsoring a foster child was more Peter's idea than Jane's. He particularly believed in helping others and paying back the benefit of a comfortable life which they were able to have. Also, in his heart and mind Peter was the perennial teacher who was always ready for a new student in his life. He came alive with the opportunity to teach.

As his student, I began guitar lessons. The placement of my fingers on the neck of the guitar seemed impossible for me to master. He then brought out cameras and lamps and taught me some basics of photography and lighting which I enjoyed.

When we were planning a driving trip across the country, he gave me the task of studying the US map and charting our course. This proved to be too boring to hold my attention. When alone in the house I would sit at the piano and pretend I knew how to play by experimenting with the keyboard.

Peter especially was in tune with me. He noticed when I was feeling a little off. Most often I was able to hide my anxiety and tears by going to my room. Confused, I cried myself to sleep often. On those few times I could not get to my room, Peter took the time to just sit and be with me. One time when he had driven me to school, I froze up in front of the school, had tears streaming down my face and felt too paralyzed to get out of the car. He waited patiently for what seemed like hours. Finally, he asked if I wanted to go back home. I spent the rest of the day in my room frightened, confused, and crying. These mood changes which I could not seem to control were very unsettling as I had always managed to maintain control. Peter did not intervene or ask any questions.

Jane, who was warm and gracious, showed her affection somewhat differently. Children are perceptive and intuitive. Even at the age of 16 this was true for me. I could sense her gentle heart reach out to me. At the same time, there was a certain guardedness. It was not until I became a young mother that I understood how bonded a mother is to her own children. One day while driving across the Bay Bridge with Jane from visiting the Vorpal Gallery in San Francisco, I managed to bring up the subject of being a mother and the feeling of bonding between mother and child which felt like no other relationship. I acknowledged Jane for accepting me with such a kind and warm open heart. I acknowledged that I knew and understood that while her feelings for me were special, deep and genuine, I also knew that they were not identical to those feelings she had for Ann and Michael. I told her that I totally understood. I shared with her that I could sense her guardedness when she, Ann or Michael and I were all together. I told her that I did not think it took anything away from our relationship, just that our relationship was different in a special way. With the difficulty of a throat too choked to speak, I confessed that I felt guilty for what was becoming clear of Ann's difficulties in navigating life. Jane sweetly tried to assure me that I had nothing to do with Ann's problems; that Ann had been a 'high-octane' child from a tender age. She described Ann as demanding, commanding, and dramatically creative. She added that Ann was difficult to understand, let alone handle. She told of the times when Ann would present a play that she had created in her head. She described vividly how Ann would play all the parts. Ann would summon everyone who was there to be her captive audience. If anyone's attention seemed to wander with chatter, Ann would stop, stomp her foot and tell that person to pay attention to her. Jane said she found Ann's plays very amusing and fascinating in how she seemed to create from out of space and execute as though she had rehearsed for months. Jane was proud of and amused by Ann but also, she confessed, stymied, and exhausted as Ann's mother.

In contrast to Ann, Jane told of how Michael was never anything but sweet and gentle. She said she could put him in the playpen next to her and he was content to just lie or sit there by her side. The special loving, calm bond between Michael and Jane played out throughout Jane's lifetime.

Jane concluded our discussion by saying that no matter what a child born to you is like, there is a mother-heart that holds them dearly, no matter what. As a mother I can attest to that, even if we don't know how or what to do as a mother in a myriad of circumstances.

The vibe in the VW as we rode across the bay bridge became filled with a sweet fragrance of grace and compassion that reminded me of smoldering White Rose incense. Sweet.

The air of relief that I sensed from Jane was palpable as she briefly confirmed that yes, the bond between a mother and her child is uniquely special and unlike any other relationship. Jane thanked me for opening the space for sharing and for understanding. That day our love and respect for each other became affirmed on a deeper and unique level.

Jane was refined and dignified in every way. Because she had majored in English at college and was a writer, I became her special project for speaking English properly. I found this confusing because I had always gotten top grades in English. It seemed that every time I spoke, she corrected my speech. This contributed to my crying myself to sleep at night, believing she no longer liked me or really wanted me there. High anxiety was taking over the feelings of being safe. I worried that this was turning 'sour', as Dr. MacCleod had repeated like a mantra so often.

As it turned out, I have forever learned and affirmed with deep gratitude that Jane's correcting my speech was the most precious gift she, or anyone, could have given to me and which has made the most profoundly priceless difference in all aspects of my entire life.

Jane's project regarding my proper speaking ability must have spurred questions on Peter's mind. Peter took it upon himself to schedule a meeting with my high school counselor to go over my schedule of classes. Although he knew what classes I was taking, he used this as an excuse to sit with Miss Mullen, my high school counselor. Miss Mullin acknowledged that I was not taking college-prep classes because she felt I was not college material. He assured her I was and that whatever indices she used to measure this were the result of having come from an underprivileged background thus far. He assured her that I could and would be able to be accepted into college.

Together, Peter and Miss Mullen changed my classes. To this point no one had ever really paid any attention to my school, report cards or any extracurricular activities I participated in at school, if any.

At the appropriate time, Peter drove me to San Francisco where I took my SAT test and later became enrolled in San Francisco State College.

Celeinne Ysunza, PhD

Being deeply grateful for and influenced by my two favorite teachers, Herb Wong and Betty Wilson, I felt I wanted to be a teacher of psychology.

Was it serendipitous that the first Broadway play Jane and I went to see in New York was PYGMALION?

> "The sweet spring night
> Of cherry blossom viewing
> Has ended," BASHO

CHAPTER FIFTEEN

Deep Dive Into A Pool of Despair

"Wake up!" "Wake up!"

Someone was screaming in my ear while slapping my face. I could not wake up. The voice seemed far away and unrelated. I felt like I was being dragged from some deep, dark unknown space. For that tiny moment, I could hear, but my body felt like lead. It was too heavy to move. A sea of blackness enveloped all of me as I sunk deeper. What happened after that, I do not remember.

The catalyst for an exceptionally long and profound journey had been set into motion with more seriousness than had been the many years of various study and therapy sessions I had undertaken in search of myself and the answers to life. Also, it became clear that my goal had been for the purpose of searching and studying was to validate myself, to feel whole and worthy. A very brief failed marriage and feeling totally overwhelmed with the responsibility of two young children did not help. Feelings of suffocation were engulfing me once again.

Greater than the shame at what had taken place was the overwhelming feeling of needing to be present and whole for my two young children whom I wanted and loved. Feeling completely alone, overwhelmed, unworthy as a parent and desperately frantic for my children and their successful development, it was obvious that professional therapy was needed. I wanted to have children very much and more than that, I wanted to give them the loving, safe, and nurturing home that I did not get for the first 16 years of my life. Although they were my everything, my all., it became painfully clear that I had no idea regarding parenting skills. I knew that love was the main ingredient, and I knew I loved them. How that translates as a parent, I had no clue. I felt spent and empty, running on thin fumes.

One day I noticed a book on a co-worker's desk. It was Gina Cerminara's, <u>Many Mansions</u>. Co-worker, Joe, noticed that I was taken by the book. He said it was a fascinating read, asking if I wanted to borrow it. Gratefully I accepted. When I got home that evening there was a book in my mailbox from Peter. It was a new copy of <u>Many Mansions</u>. His note explained that he felt 'driven' to get that book for me because he thought I might find it interestingly insightful.

No one has ever known of my previous suicide attempt except for the one close friend who had the strong intuitive thought to intervene and call 911. I had asked her to babysit for me while I ran errands. She said she could sense something was not right. After I was released from the hospital, she took me and the children into her home for a while as I got reoriented and back into my work and parenting routine.

"You can't forgive without loving. And I don't mean sentimentality. I don't mean mush. I mean having enough courage to stand up and say, 'I forgive. I'm finished with it." Maya Angelou

Exhausted from overwhelming depression and high anxiety for my children, my life felt like it was a ball of yarn unraveling downhill, gaining momentum. I had no one to turn to. The children's father was not interested in being involved with them, let alone with me. Jane and Peter were in transition to relocate to British Columbia.

A profound dream enveloped me one night. "You see how it is all just a dream, a play…" The deep baritone voice startled me out of my sleep. I felt the presence of his strong arm around my shoulder. I looked to the right to see who this was. Nothing and no one was there. Darkness. Silence. Then I heard the word, "CUT!" Repeatedly and with increasing volume the word, 'CUT!" boomed louder and louder. I looked around again to see WHO was this man shouting at me. There was no man. There was no one.

Suddenly, I found myself in a theater, situated as though hovering above the stage where there was a young girl dressed in a pinafore dress, apron and pilgrim-style hat. Next to her was a wooden stool and butter churner. The girl just stood there crying, louder and louder. She seemed frozen. She obviously could not hear the shouts of CUT! as they became louder and louder. The voice returned to me and said, "You see how deeply attached she is to her drama on the stage? She cannot hear the cue that it is a role, a scene and that it is now over." Instantly, I was in the body of the little girl, trembling and sobbing while too frozen to move. Again, I felt the same presence with its strong arm around my shoulders guide me off the stage. The deep baritone voice continued to talk as he guided me off the stage, but I could not hear what he was saying. I was still sobbing. I remember exiting toward the right of the stage, going down a few stairs and then once again I was the outside observer standing on the stage in the blinding lights, with no audience, watching the girl and a shadow of a man walk out of site. I was both the child actor and the outside observer simultaneously.

With a hard jolt, I awoke sitting straight up in my bed, sweating, and sobbing hysterically. It was a dream within a dream. I caught myself to make sure my noise did not disturb my sleeping children.

"In this world the living grow fewer. The dead increase – how much longer must I carry this body of grief?"
Ono No Konachi Japanese

73

CHAPTER SIXTEEN

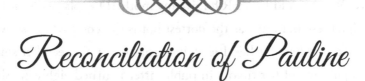

Reconciliation of Pauline

Several years later Jane and Peter introduced me to a man who had an extraordinary type of therapy that they thought could help me overcome my many painfully haunting feelings of abandonment and inadequacies as a person and, especially, as a mother.

Bob Hoffman was a good looking, short, smartly dressed man. His small office was pleasantly welcoming with drapes drawn and one lit candle. I was seated in a comfortable chair across the desk from him.

He explained that unlike other therapies I had experienced (of which there had been many and which I felt were ineffective dead ends), he was going to guide me through processes that are non-traditional but proven to have extraordinary results.

He explained that I was not going to tell him anything about my life. Rather, he was going to tell me about my life, and I was to record everything on the legal-size tablet that he placed in front of me.

Strange, I thought. He said that for this to be effective, I had to commit to one thing at the end of our sessions. That one thing was to go to visit my mother and my father, regardless of where they were in the world, and tell them I forgive them. He said that I did not have to tell them I love them; he did not want me to feel I had to love them. "You see", he said, "it is in forgiving, in lovingly divorcing ourselves from our mother and father that we become free. A higher love power takes over for you. When you are in the power of love, including for yourself, all else fades away. Any loving feelings you may feel toward your mother or father are a bonus, but don't get hung up on that and don't feel guilty if you don't feel loving feelings. Our goal is for you to lovingly release them, release the karma of bondage you share, and allow yourself to grow in heart and spirit".

NO WAY would I EVER forgive my mother! I explained that I hated her so intensely that, just as the hottest hot is the color white, so was the intensity of my hate for her. I explained that I had not seen her since she tried to pull one of her tirades in public after I turned eighteen. She had asked me to meet her at the café counter of a department store in downtown Oakland. Before our lunch could be served, she once again began a tirade against me for no apparent reason that I could understand. Feeling the power of myself being emancipated I stood from my stool and glared into her cold steely blue eyes, announcing firmly that I was an adult who never wanted to see her or hear from her again. We never again communicated. I once saw her walking toward me on the street in downtown Oakland after that incident. I quickly ducked into the Emporium and waited for her to pass.

I told Bob that I could not have cared less about her or what happened to her. If fact, I told Bob that if his therapy had to include my mother I could not proceed; that I was there for myself.

Surprisingly, Bob sat quietly watching me and listening with no response.

As for my father. I told Bob that there was nothing to forgive of my father. He was a victim of my crazy mother who took me away from him. Although I had very few memories of him, they were all gentle and good. Apparently, I was in complete denial and had dispensed with the many memories of feeling hurt, unwanted, rejected and abandoned when I had looked him up in the library and tried to contact him.

This opening session with Bob felt intensely threatening for me and left me feeling panicked and skeptical. My instinct was to leave and not look back, which was how I handled most uncomfortable and painful people and situations. He looked intently into my eyes and said that the hatred I was carrying within me was a cancer that would not only ruin all chances of any loving relationship – including with my own children – but that the hatred would surely manifest sooner or later as a cancer in my body. He said that to leave without what he had to offer me was to, in effect, sign my death warrant. Because Jane and Peter had both recommended Bob so highly, I knew this was necessary for me, as frightening as it felt.

Feeling quite certain that Pauline had died some years prior, I felt safe and relief that I would not have to face her despite the commitment Bob insisted upon. Once I reluctantly agreed and settled in to embark on the first of his sessions, Bob suddenly made a surprise announcement that he did not think he could work with me – after all that! His explanation was because he saw me living in several homes and one large institution. The premise of his therapy was to work on the relationship between the child and the biological mother and father. Regardless of how many foster parents I or anyone may have had; regardless of whether one had been adopted, his therapy was based on the spiritual/karmic blood ties of the child and its biological parents. In my case there appeared to him to be a multitude of people in the role of mother/father. I confirmed this.

After a few minutes of silence, he realized that all the other people were not my parents at all. He said that my father had "come in" (in spirit) and was very anxious to have this session. I insisted that was not possible or necessary. Impatiently, I reminded Bob that I was there for ME, not my father or my mother, both of whom were never there for me.

He assured me that I would see how this is ALL for me, and for them as well, but mainly for me. He tried to explain that by my lovingly divorcing from my mother and father, I could become healed of all the pain and traumas from my relationship with each of them which, he said, was my soul's purpose in this lifetime. He further explained that my healing would become my mother's and father's healing, just as their dysfunctional selves had become my dysfunction. He was firm in directing me to drop all thoughts of them for now to not get too distracted from the momentary process. He assured me it would be a win-win situation for me.

Many hours of sessions, many pages filled with writing told the full and accurate story of my life as recited by Bob. I found this to be quite amazing as well as exhausting. Because I did stay to complete all the sessions with Bob, I knew I then had to fulfill my commitment to find my father to offer my forgiveness. Knowing with a fair degree of certainty my mother had died I felt relieved to not have to find her and have any time with her.

The writing on the several pages of the yellow tablet unveiled the story of Pauline, who she was and what her childhood was like. My job was to confirm as much as possible with other family members. Having lived the nightmare, I could confirm her story very well. As for her childhood I could only confirm a few things that her sister, Ginny, had shared with me when she and I met briefly when I was fifteen and again when I was eighteen after she had moved to Los Angeles.

Pauline was one of five children with two sisters and two brothers. According to her sister, Pauline was considered different from an early age. Incredibly early in her childhood, Pauline earned the label as the family's black sheep which brought out the wrath of their very cold and stern father who had an old-world German background. Over the years, Pauline's behavior developed from eccentric to cruel. Perhaps this was because she couldn't get the attention and nurturing she craved and needed, perhaps because she saw that she was different and perceived as different in the eyes of her parents as compared to her siblings. Her sister told me that Pauline was expelled from school and from the family when she angrily threw acid toward another pupil in her chemistry class.

Pauline's two sisters appeared to fulfill normal lives in marriage and as parents as did her one brother who lived in Healdsburg, CA. Another brother became disconnected and lost to the family also in a void of alcoholism. This was the ex-husband of Aunt Helen and father of cousin, Bill, both of whom I loved being with that one very brief time as a toddler.

Feeling comfortable that I would not have to search for and confront Pauline, I became shocked back into a certain reality when Bob surprised me with the announcement that Pauline was present, in spirit. Instantly I froze with fear. All breath was sucked from me. I was too afraid to move. Like a high priest, Bob performed what he called a cleansing and releasing ceremony between me and Pauline.

Amazingly, at the end of Bob's process there was no fear or sadness filling me. My heart felt like melted butter with compassion for her and what was obviously the wretched life she had lived. Like me, Pauline seemed to have had a lonely and fearful childhood that made her escape into alcohol and anger. A swift arctic cold wind felt like it was passing through Pauline's and my history flashing before me as though I was an observer watching a movie being played in a fast forward mode. I was absolutely and totally an unattached observer. Once again, I could breathe.

A new type of pain filled my heart. I felt compassion for Pauline without any trace of an emotional charge or trigger. She had become a totally fictional stranger in a movie script. As with any good movie, I did become temporarily caught up in the intensity of the drama with all the emotions and tears. Bob's processes were like walking outside the movie theater into the afternoon light, realizing that it was a very good movie that managed to hold me captive, but that it was not 'real', it was just a movie.

Although the emotional charge between us was discharged, it was important for me that she knew my words of forgiveness were true and genuinely from my heart. This was and is my native and inherent nature;

Celeinne Ysunza, PhD

to feel deeply for another's pain and a desire to help them alleviate that pain. We concluded with a prayer.

Like magic Pauline and I were absolutely and totally two very individual strangers with no sense of connection whatsoever. Pauline left. Exactly as she had done over and over in our physical lifetime. Once again, the feeling of an extremely heavy weight from a tremendous boulder lifted from me and I felt like I could breathe. Yes. Always struggling for air.

CHAPTER SEVENTEEN

Enduring Odyssey of Forgiveness

Surprisingly, Frank, with whom I declared to Bob I had no issues and thus no reason to forgive, proved to be not so accurate. With Bob's gentle guidance he helped me face the scars of having been rejected by Frank multiple times. His absence, his silence and his turning his back on me left me deeply imprinted with feelings of abandonment, of not being worthy of love and acceptance.

Trust issues had consumed me all my life, especially when it came to the opposite sex. Looking back at earlier love relationships I could see that I was attracted to men who were emotionally unavailable and in their own way, rejected or abandoned me. When I did have someone who really was kind and loving, as I had very early before my first marriage, I refused to accept that I was loved because I didn't believe I was lovable. Running, running was the name of the game when it came to these relationships.

Bob showed me how Frank's behavior became the blueprint of how I would relate to men in my life. He showed me that the experience of being neglected and abandoned was a huge detriment to love relationships.

Honoring the initial contractual commitment with Bob involved going to wherever in the world each parent was in order to forgive them. It was time to, once again, visit the local public library to see if Frank was still listed in the phone book for Pittsburgh, Pennsylvania. He was. Again, I found this amazing given that he had so often asked me not to contact him.

Uncertain as to whether he would accept my call or hang up, I asked a male friend to hold the phone until Frank answered. Once it was confirmed he was Frank, my friend handed the phone to me. When I said hello and who I was, there was a pregnant pause. I was sure he was going to hang up. Clearing his throat, he asked me how I was, to which I replied that I was fine. He then asked how my mother was. I told him I hadn't seen or talked with her in many years, but I was pretty sure she had deceased, probably from cirrhosis of the liver. He said that she had contacted him several years earlier to ask for money for an operation which he was not able to do. It struck me as strange that Pauline would have contacted Frank for money for an operation that may have saved her life.

I asked Frank if he would be willing and able to meet me for just a couple hours in the Pittsburgh airport in two weeks. He quickly changed our conversation into a cryptic business conversational tone saying that he would have to check his calendar with his secretary the next day and get back to me, asking for my phone number. Of course, I said yes. With trepidation, a heavy heart and tears I hung up knowing I would never hear from him again. Had I lovingly divorced myself from Frank, I wondered.

The next evening at 6:30 the phone rang. It was Frank. He apologized for having to make the call sound like a business call. He explained that he had a wife who knows nothing about me. This was his third wife with whom he had no other children.

We confirmed the potential flight I was to reserve from San Francisco on a Friday night red eye that would land in Pittsburgh early Saturday morning. He asked again how I was. I told him I was fine, had a respectable job and had two beautiful children that I was hoping he could meet one day. I assured him that my intentions were genuine. I let him know that I would book a return flight to California two hours after the initial landing in Pittsburgh.

Whether or not Frank would show up to meet me at the airport in Pittsburgh, PA felt risky, but I had to fulfill this process, my final step and commitment with Bob and myself. As we were about to end the call, he asked me how we would recognize each other. I told him that one of the things Pauline always seemed so angry about was that I looked so much like him. I had seen pictures of him so I felt we would not have any problem finding each other.

Feeling overwhelmed with extreme anxiety, my head began to spin, my stomach churn and I felt stunned with pain in my eyes and ears. I hung up the phone, went to the bathroom to throw up and then crawled under the covers with a pillow over my head.

The positive final experience I had with Pauline in Bob's session left no doubt in my mind that a journey of forgiveness with Frank was equally important. In fact, I knew it was going to be much easier as I did not have the years of frightening violent trauma with him as I had with Pauline.

The night before I was to leave for the San Francisco airport, I explained to my children that I would be back later Saturday afternoon and that our friend would be staying with them until I returned.

Feeling as though I was in a strange dream state, I walked into the airport terminal after getting off the plane early Saturday morning. I saw the tall, large-framed man that I recognized as Frank approaching me. He recognized me immediately. Strangely, we did not hug. The airport seemed spookily empty of people and the usual hustle and bustle of an airport.

It appeared that we were the only two people there, floating toward each other in slow motion. Very surreal. Feeling somewhat anxious I noticed another, deeper, sense of relief and joy at presenting him with the gift of forgiveness and to see that I really was OK so that he could release any guilt he may be harboring (which Bob said he had). I assume that could be a good guess on anybody's part. Bob also told me he was taking medications for his heart.

After confirming my return flight at the ticket counter, Frank and I found a quiet remote spot in the airport to visit. Frank was dressed in a suit and bowtie. I noticed that his full head of hair was almost black. I knew he was a redhead as was I. He had an air of Victorian decorum. He seemed vulnerable and uncomfortable at the very emotional meeting. Awkwardly he fumbled with superficialities as he complimented me on how nice I looked. He then asked why I chose to fly across the country to see him. The air of fear or despair around Frank was heavy. I told him that it was important he know that I was well, a successfully functioning working single mother of two and, mainly, that I wanted him to know that he did not need to have any worries or feelings of guilt about his not being there for and with me. Holding his hand, I shared that I knew our living across the country from each other made any visits impossible, but that I understood.

Tears began to well in Frank's eyes. With a choked voice that needed clearing he told me that he had anguished for years with guilt over not helping me all the times I reached out to him. He was clearly begging for my compassionate forgiveness. He explained that he had a failed second marriage with two sons; that he was currently in a third marriage with no other children. His trembling hands popped several pills in his mouth, explaining that they were for anxiety and a heart condition. Feeling the effects of sleep deprivation, I fought lightheadedness knowing I had to maintain this intense connection; it seemed vital to Frank. My purpose in being there was to give the gift of forgiveness to Frank.

Frank appeared to have an urgent need to paint for me a personal identity of himself and his accomplishments. He told me that he had gone back to college on the VA bill to get his degree in civil engineering. He was clearly proud of his well-to-do earnings as a salesperson for a major company that makes heavy duty farm equipment. He was so pleased to have finally been able to drive the car of his dreams, a Cadillac. He described his home and neighborhood. I saw a perfectly manicured Normal Rockwell scene. He was especially proud to have been voted successive terms as Mayor of his Borough.

When I asked Frank to share a little about his mother and father, he seemed very vulnerable and guarded. Frank shared that he was the only son of the three children in his family. He described his mother as very English, Victorian, aloof, not affectionate. His stern German father and he never had a good relationship. I remember visiting their house one time when I was very young. Frank left me with them for some reason. I remember there were several potted plants all around the living room and a singing canary. I remember his father retreating completely to another room. He never came out and never talked with me. Frank's mother busied herself with no real interaction with me either. Not sure why Frank had deposited me with his parents, I felt uncomfortably alien, invisible and anxious to have Frank return to take me out of there.

His two sisters each had one marriage compared to Frank's three marriages. He seemed wrapped in an aura of sadness. I told him that a few years earlier I had written a twenty-two-page typed letter to him and sent it to his mother to deliver to him. He said he never received it.

The two hours that were originally planned for the visit flew faster than either of us could fathom. When the time to leave grew close, Frank begged me to see if I could catch a later flight home to stay with him a little longer. I changed my flight to a later flight and called home to let my friend and children know.

He said he was anxious to build a relationship with me and his two grandchildren. He said he would plan a business trip to San Francisco in order to visit us and meet his grandchildren. Concerned about the financial hardship of buying a ticket to see him, he offered to send me a check to cover the airfare.

Four hours later, totally exhausted, I boarded the plane for San Francisco. Looking out the window while waiting for takeoff I saw a strange blob of something outside floating slowly toward me as though it was going to penetrate the window. Whatever it was, it floated right up to the window where I could see clearly what it was. I was totally unaware of where I was, the many people boarding or the person who sat next to me. I felt a distinct lightness of body. I had not had a full night's sleep since Thursday night. Slowly, very slowly, an exquisitely beautiful butterfly emerged from the blob. The blob was a cocoon! That was the last thing I remember before being awakened by the pilot's voice five or six hours later that announced our arrival into the San Francisco International Airport.

A few weeks later Frank sent me a letter with a check for $25.00 stating that he would send the rest to me in installments. Because he wanted to maintain our connection and because his wife didn't know about me, he opened a post office mailbox in another person's name in Ohio (one of his weekly business stopovers) so that I could write to him.

Frank did manage to come to San Francisco for business and stay with us at our apartment in San Jose. His letters became less and less frequent. My letters to him became infrequent. What I found fascinating was my perception and expectation of Frank in our "new" relationship. No longer did I have any anticipation of hearing from him. I was curious to see if he would keep his commitment to build a relationship and send any more checks for the airfare. I felt I wanted to just be there for him if he needed our connection. I tentatively held the hope for my children that he would form a relationship with them for their sake.

Contrary to what I think Frank believed, I didn't feel he had a genuine intention of a real connection with me or his grandchildren. There was no substance, no conscious memory upon which to build a bridge. It was a very strange sensation of what is called the No-thing.

This was a surreal experience.

Within months of completing my processes with Bob Hoffman I discovered that I had stage three cancer of the uterus and cervix. Once I had recovered from surgery, I wrote to Frank to tell him that I had not written because I had undergone cancer surgery, but that I was okay.

Like a phone that goes dead, there was never any more communication between Frank and me. I wondered if he had died.

CHAPTER EIGHTEEN

Lotus Heart Unfolding

With heartfelt compassion for Frank and Pauline, a feeling of peace coursed through my being. I could feel the expansive warmth of sunshine, the fragrance of flowers, hear the birds singing and, most importantly, I could breathe freely. With this new experience of deep genuine forgiveness and compassion for Frank and Pauline, the ecstasy of freedom embraced me. No thoughts. No fear. No hatred. No regrets. Just the warmth of overflowing love. I couldn't even begin to explain exactly what had transpired, only how I felt. Pure delightful and inspirational magic.

At the end of my sessions with Bob I realized in my heart that Frank and Pauline were, like so many of us, two painfully damaged children trapped in an adult body trying to maintain a sense of equilibrium that would help them cope while bearing their individual sacks of pain, unresolved issues and everyday challenges for survival. Like most of us, Frank and Pauline arrived on the world stage appearing as adults because of their biological/ physical appearance. As adults, there no longer was available to them the compassion that is expressed for young, vulnerable children or for animals. As adults they, like most of us, were expected to be complete, upright, mentally and emotionally responsible citizens living in a concrete jungle. Like many of us, they were clueless, not knowing what they did not know, just trying to survive while fencing with their unique demons.

That most precious aspect of themselves, their inner child, was deeply damaged. Their inner child had been abandoned and left crying and crying out to be held and loved. What about their parents' and grandparents' lives and demons?

It is with unconditional love, or at least non-judgement, and supportive shepherding that the child can develop into a strong and whole adult. Being adults physically doesn't mean we are adults emotionally or spiritually. Even if I do not know with certainty as much about the childhood traumas Pauline and Frank may have experienced, my heart ached for them knowing that they were trying to shake the demon monkeys from their own backs in order to simply survive from drowning in their own private personal abyss. It is very complex at the level of the earthling.

I left Bob Hoffman's office knowing that my journey with Bob Hoffman and his unique and unorthodox processes were totally successful. I had lovingly divorced myself from each of my birth parents. Who was I to judge their life, their pain and sorrow or how they did or did not balance all the issues while maintaining their way along the path of life?

Absolutely no charge whatsoever exists for me relative to Pauline or Frank. This is all thanks to Bob's incredible talent and process. No longer any feelings of expectations at all; no good, no bad and, nothing in between. It was truly transformational and liberating beyond words.

Over the years Bob Hoffman went on to expand his Transformational Process into the remarkably successful Hoffman Institute International, implementing what is known as The Hoffman Process.

Many years later I met a lady with whom I became friends. She told me about an awesome therapy process she had experienced and invited me to join her at a dinner presentation honoring the founder of this process which was to be held in Napa Valley. When I asked her to tell me more about the therapist and process, she said she had undergone an intensive workshop at the Hoffman Institute, founded by Bob Hoffman.

When she explained that she was part of a large group, I told her I was one of Bob's early clients; that his process was very uniquely done on a one-on-one process and I couldn't imagine how he could possibly have done that as a large group or train others to guide the process. She said she couldn't see how he could work one on one.

The event honoring Bob Hoffman took place sometime in the mid 1990's. As one of his early clients, I was excited to meet him so many years later. As it turned out, Bob was too ill to attend the event. He passed on before there could be another event or opportunity to meet him again.

"As the caterpillar, having come to the end of one blade of grass, draws itself together and reaches out for the next, so the Self, having come to the end of one life and shed all ignorance, gathers in its faculties and reaches out from the old body to a new." *(Brihadaranyaka III.4.3)* <u>The Upanishads</u> Eknath Easwaran

During his process with me, Bob interspersed ideas and philosophies about karma; that we each are chosen to fulfill a higher purpose. Sometimes the road is long and hard but, he said, "Know that you will never be given more than your soul is ready to endure for God knows you better than you and will always guide and protect you lovingly." He was insistent about teaching the positive healing power of forgiveness and compassion, not only for others; for oneself as well. With gentle compassion he told me that, yes, I had chosen my parents and life script and it was my purpose to learn to forgive and let go without any judgement or criticalness. That created a piercing sting in my heart because I had been extremely judgmental and critical of most people and things in my life. My survival mechanism had been honed sharply by judging and criticizing.

Hearing this thought expressed on such a personal level from Bob left my head spinning. Reading this concept intellectually and having it applied to me personally was not what I was prepared to accept. I cannot say that I was totally sold this early in my journey; on the idea that I could have chosen Pauline and Frank or the life script that came with them. My intellect brain could not accept that anyone would choose all that pain and craziness. My survival mode had built intricate castles within that made me feel less vulnerable. Compassionate forgiveness for Pauline and Frank was a grand release of stuffed and pent-up negative emotions; a 'la petite mort'. The Sufi poet, Rumi, said, "Out beyond ideas of wrongdoing and right doing, there is a field. I will meet you there."

There is an anonymous quote, "Forgiveness is giving up the hope for a better past". Check. All the old negative garbage emotions that had been released from the darkest depths of my inner self rose as smudge smoke in the air.

From the vestiges of the old ugly and scratchy burlap of negative thoughts, emotions and reactions a new garb spewed forth; the shimmering cloak of egoic haughtiness at having overcome my childhood circumstances. In my mind/universe I knew that no one had suffered as badly as I had in childhood. This is the epitome of believing that we are a Self, separate and apart from each other. Ah, hah! The trickster of the mind had changed his dance to fool me into participating with him in a new form of dance!

This was the next necessary steppingstone for the unfoldment of my consciousness. I had not yet truly experienced my consciousness as also Pauline and Frank's consciousness as well as my husband's and children's consciousness. I had not yet experienced a deeper level of knowing that Nature's work is perfect. The size, shape and timing of unfoldment are all precisely perfect for each of us and each of our individual as well as wholistic, collective chapters in history. Like a big, beautiful spider web we are woven from the same silk of supreme consciousness. When there is a vibration from movement anywhere on the web, the effects of the vibrations are felt throughout the entire network. I was to learn how the movement of vibration and sound manifest from the quality of my own as well as one tiny aspect of the collective mind consciousness.

There are no voids. It is said that the nature of the archetypal center (Self) is to undergo cyclic rounds of birth, death and resurrection.

For the Western world who does not believe in reincarnation, the new age psychologists and psychiatrists can guide their patient to see that the philosophies of the East, mysticism and metaphysics, as well as Judeo/

Christian practices relate to our psychospiritual self. Like the snake we shed the old which has been outgrown to not suffocate us and that no longer serves the highest good of mankind on his journey home.

The people of archaic and ancient cultures who were the high priests and shamans understood this. We in this modern, materialistic cycle have become far removed from their wisdoms much as an untethered raft drifts far from shore. We are hypnotized by the glitter of the false gold in linear thought and time. We believe we are superior at navigating the higher power of the cyclic world of Nature.

Stanislav Grof, MD, PhD, says in his book, The Cosmic Game, "The divine play is not a completely closed system; it offers the protagonists the possibility to discover the true nature of creation, including their own cosmic status". [pg. 182-183]

The childhood hangover, a fanciful myth, in the belief of being protectively surrounded by and somewhat guided by beings of a higher order had not abandoned me completely. Hanging on by the skin of my fingernails much of my life meant that I had to find an anchor, any anchor that would keep me here for the sake of my children. Otherwise, I could have landed in the hospital where Pauline should have been. My body was too sensitive to tolerate alcohol or drugs, probably as a result of Pauline's drunkenness during her pregnancy. The path has slowly unfurled for me to become blessed with the wisdom of many great teachers, schools and people including my husband, his children and my children. And it is slowly becoming clear that, while all the book knowledge is good and helpful, it is only by surrendering to the Higher Source, God, Jesus or whatever is your label; then going within during meditation. This is an invitation from our heart-temple that turns on the light. In this light there truly is no room for judgement.

There is no destination, only the eternal journey with some rest stops, some mountains and much wealth bestowed as gifts of lessons of entanglement, darkness into light, light into darkness.

"There's no getting ready, other than grace. My faults have stayed hidden; One might call that preparation! There are so many threats to it. Inside of us, there's a continual autumn. Our leaves fall and are blown out over the water. A crow sits in the blackened limbs and talks about what's gone." The Illuminated Rumi [Translated by Coleman Barks]

I was to later realize that this one little act of forgiveness in life was not the end-all or cure for pain and suffering in our life. It was only the beginning. I understood what the Buddhist monk, Pema Chodron, meant when she said, "If we learn to open our hearts, anyone, including the people who drive us crazy, can be our teachers."

CHAPTER NINETEEN

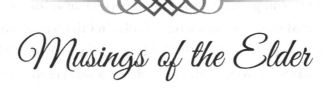

Musings of the Elder

Now, as an elder living among other elders, I watch them and wonder about their life gains, pains and lessons and silently bless them that they are feeling at peace with the grand movie script they authored, directed and starred in. My prayerful intention for them is that they do not feel lonely or guilty; that they and their loved ones are reconciled before the leaves fall from their family tree this season for them. My heart now lives with them, knowing we are not separate. We are spiritual warriors working as a collective unit for the ongoing unfoldment and higher good of mankind. I know that the karmas we have burned off has been replaced by the karmas of the children and grandchildren. Spirals within spirals are the movement of life eternally and infinitely.

Living among and witnessing elders who are often rescued from falls or ailments and, of course, exiting their final chapter, brings Pauline to my mind occasionally. Although my forgiveness of her is complete, I feel a pang in my heart for her realizing that she probably died all alone in some dank room. Knowing she had cirrhosis of the liver, she probably had a painful transition. I have forgiven myself for not being strong enough or courageous enough to be there to take care of her as my sweet nephew had done with his mother, Ann.

My heart's intention is that whatever is my soul growth and unfoldment, so is Pauline's soul and growth development. We no longer need to dance together the Lila upon the wheel of Samsara for this to be accomplished, for it is already so. I have learned to be grateful for the tremendous wealth of lessons through Pauline and Frank in this life script knowing we are complete, thanks to Bob Hoffman and his process along with the multitude of subsequent teachers who have graced my life.

Most significantly, my husband particularly, has been an unwavering epitome of graceful patience, love and support, often at his own expense. He has fulfilled many previously voided roles in this lifetime, not only for me but for so many including my children and his ex-wife's siblings and family. He has been an eternally gentle flame, a shaman to many.

My children suffered the loss of solid parenting and, also, have had to find strength within. As their mother, their shepherd, they have shown me their unwavering love, acceptance and respect. Just as I with Pauline and Frank had a destiny to fulfill, so do I with my children as they have with me and within themselves.

Pierre Tielhard de Chardin, the French Jesuit Priest, describes our time here as "Fulfilling the Grand Opus Magnum."

Knowing there are no destinations, only journeys, I ask deeply each day for guidance from above for continued healing, compassionate patience, strength, and courage.

St. Francis of Assisi said, "There are beautiful and wild forces within us."

Rumi expanded upon that with, "If you put your soul against this oar with me, the power that made the universe will enter your sinew from a source not outside your limbs, but from a holy realm that lives in us." Secrets of the Lost Mode of Prayer Gregg Braden

Periodically, circumstances in my life along this journey of self-forgiveness and self-acceptance seem more daunting than forgiveness of Pauline and Frank.

Spirals within spirals. As tiny aspects of the One, we continue ever upward together as aspects of each other fulfilling the Grand Opus Magnum for the collective of mankind.

Om mane padme hum.

In your heart there is a lotus
In the lotus there is a jewel
In the jewel is the
Source of Life.

Printed in the United States
by Baker & Taylor Publisher Services